To Ian
Thanks for insp...

From Sea to Shining Sea

One woman's cycle trip across Canada from Mile 0 in
British Columbia to Mile 0 in Newfoundland

Patti Kagawa

Victoria, BC Canada

P Kagawa

Maps and Cover by Kai Fuglem
Cover photograph: Kootenay Lake, B.C. at sunset
Cover photograph of author: Susan Zedel

Library and Archives Canada Cataloguing in Publication

Kagawa, Patti, 1956-
    From sea to shining sea : one woman's cycle trip across Canada from Mile 0 in British Columbia to Mile 0 in Newfoundland / Patti Kagawa.

Includes bibliographical references.
ISBN 978-0-9869367-0-8

    1. Kagawa, Patti, 1956- --Travel--Canada. 2. Canada--Description and travel. 3. Bicycle touring--Canada. I. Title.

FC76.K33 2011   917.104'73   C2011-903690-8

Log House Press; www.loghousepress.ca
Printorium Bookworks, a division of Island Blue
Victoria, British Columbia, Canada

Dedication

Dedicated to all those people who say, "I've always wanted to cycle across the country," and to inspire them to go for it.

Table of Contents

Acknowledgements

Thank you to all those who cycled alongside of me, both in training and on the journey: Kerri Brownie, Nancy Densmore, Jen Erlendson, Barb Gosling, Denise McGowan, Sheila Rogers, Leah Saville, Susan Zedel and lastly, my daughter, Naomi Fuglem, who had just turned 16 at the time and truly went outside her comfort zone to accompany me on the last leg of the trip.

To all the friendly strangers and friends who provided food, accommodation, rides and hospitality, thank you for your help to make this trip so much more pleasurable. Many of your names are in the book. Without your kind assistance, the trip would have been a much tougher slog.

Thank you to all those who helped edit this manuscript: Rex Frost, Susan Frost, Nancy Densmore, Ian Leung and especially Jen Erlendson who kept pestering me to write this book. I am very grateful to Esther Hart of Author Solutions who wordsmithed alongside of me to achieve the final version.

Disclaimer

This book is designed to provide information on planning and accomplishing a cycling trip across the country. It is sold with the understanding that the publisher and author are not engaged in rendering legal or accounting services. If legal or other expert assistance is required, the services of a competent professional should be sought. This information is based on the author's own experience cycling across the country. It is not the purpose of this book to reprint all the information that is otherwise available to readers but to complement, simplify and pass on the author's first hand cycling experience.

Every effort has been made to make this book as complete and accurate as possible. This book should be used only as a general guide and, as the author is human, there may unwittingly be errors. The purpose of this book is to inspire you to plan and accomplish a cycling trip of your dreams. Any ordinary person with a passion to cycle tour can accomplish this. You are encouraged to research all the available material about cycle touring and cycling in the area you choose.

The author and publishing company shall have neither liability nor responsibility to any person or entity with respect to any loss or damage caused, or alleged to have been caused, directly or indirectly, by the information contained in this book.

If you do not wish to be bound by the above, you may return this book to the publisher for a full refund.

Introduction

Who can cycle across Canada?

If you

- want to see the country,
- are determined, focused and like a challenge and
- enjoy cycling, are interested in cycle touring and are comfortable riding a bike,

you are a likely candidate.

Canada is a vast country, full of wondrous sights and inspiring people. It may take a while but if you have the time, cycling is an ideal way to travel and view the country at ground level (literally). Cycling into a town loaded down with panniers is a great conversation starter, in any language. Luckily, English across the country is the same (except for accents) and if you find a French ambassador or if you remember even a bit of that old high school French, you can survive in Québec and other French-speaking areas. Canadians across the land are friendly, curious, helpful, empathetic and hospitable.

This book is meant to inspire readers to find a challenge that suits them and help give them the determination to accomplish it. It is not a cycle touring guidebook, but a general guidebook to cycling across Canada. The travelogue part of this book is based on a journal that I tried to write in every day. It uses some short forms (translated at the back) and shortened sentences as part of the writing style.

Chapter 1
Preparation

Planning

It all started in early 2007 when I was reading the newspaper editorials, as I like to do. One columnist was waxing lyrically about life. He basically said that life is too short and there is no point waiting until retirement to do the things you really want to do. He made me think, "He's right....what am I waiting for?" It helps me to have a challenge, to have something to train for. My challenge would be to cycle across Canada, from Mile 0 in Victoria, British Columbia to Mile 0 in St. John's, Newfoundland. It just so happened that my brother and sister-in-law and family were moving to St. John's and I had always wanted to visit Newfoundland. They had lived there previously but moved to Edmonton before I had a chance to get there. Here was my chance—quick before they moved elsewhere again. All I had to do was get agreement from my husband, my teenage children (or maybe convince them to join me!) and my employer.

There are many websites and books on this type of venture. I perused them and became convinced that I would be able to meet this challenge, given enough time. When I started mentioning my idea to friends and they didn't think I was totally insane, it gave me hope. Following others' experience, I determined that I would need about three months to allow myself enough time to get from coast to coast. My deadline was to return in time to give my co-workers a holiday in August, so that meant starting by May 1. Approval from all the parties involved was obtained in the summer of 2007.

Training

Fortunately, there were a few fellow female adventurers in Victoria who decided to join me for various legs of this challenge. Jen, Susan, Nancy and Leah decided the winter before the trip that they would train with me, which certainly motivated me even more. By November, I had bought a new touring bicycle, specialized for carrying the weight of fully loaded panniers. Before the December holidays, we started organizing cycling gear. Jen decided to try using her current road racing bike and using a BOB (brand name) trailer to carry her gear. She continued to tour with the same and eventually had to upgrade her gears to assist hill climbing. Please see the "Decisions, Decisions" section at the back for details on some decisions made.

Training rides were a chance to challenge ourselves and to get to know our neighbourhoods. As well, we got to know each other and, importantly, got used to our bike saddles. Day trips included 70 km trips to Sooke and back, 70 km trips around the Saanich peninsula and others through some steep hills in the Highlands region around Victoria. One weekend Jen and I tested our new lightweight tents in the howling winds off Saltspring Island's Ruckle Park. We learned how to ride in a group using hand signals and learned the need for adequate food, rest and water. In reality, the real training for

12

the steep and long climbs of BC's mountain passes was actually cycling through them.

A few of us took a very short course on increasing our knowledge of the most basic bike repairs: how to fix a flat tire, how to fix a broken chain, how to replace a broken spoke, how to change brake or gear cables and how to use a mini tire pump. As well as cycling, it is a good idea to practise these repairs in case of emergency.

Chapter 2
The Journey through British Columbia

Day 1, Thursday, May 1
Mile 0, Victoria, BC
Distance: 73 km to White Rock, BC

Jen, Leah and I at the Mile 0 marker at Victoria, BC; Day 1

Jen, Leah and I met at the Mile 0 marker to have our photos taken before walking down to touch our hands in the Pacific Ocean. This was the start of a long journey for us and we had many family and friends in tow to see us depart. We stopped for an inspirational moment by the Terry Fox memorial statue near the Mile 0 marker in Beacon Hill Park then said a huge goodbye to the many folks who had come to send us off. We eagerly started cycling with a contingent of friends: Susan, Brian and Steve, who had to return to work soon after. We were excited by a sense of adventure mixed with some trepidation by finally commencing this trip after the six months of talking, training and planning. The three of us, Jen, Leah and I, continued cycling along Hwy 17 north to the BC Ferries Swartz Bay terminal. The ferry fare for bicycles was reasonable and the ferry provided very secure and practical bike racks, made for touring bicycles to ensure they wouldn't move around. The bonus was bicycles were the first on and off the ferry, ahead of the car traffic. The 1½ hour break in the middle of cycle touring was a pleasant opportunity to eat and relax.

Once off the ferry, we were into new territory along the highway from the Tsawwassen ferry terminal. We followed highway 17 to Hwy 99A South, took Exit 10 to White Rock and then followed MapQuest instructions to the luxurious residence where friends, Susan and Lyle, fed and housed us. We were so lucky to have such deluxe accommodation on Day 1. Our host, Susan, then drove us on a preview route through White Rock, along the very scenic Marine Drive, then east towards (but bypassing) the Peace Arch border crossing and towards 0 Avenue. We participated in a fundraiser for the Make a Wish Foundation at the ABC Country Restaurant at White Rock. We treated Susan and Jenny (Susan's daughter) to some extravagant desserts in support of the cause, before heading back to their house.

Day 2, Friday, May 2
Distance: 87 km to Cultus Lake Provincial Park; rolling hills

We said thank you and goodbye to our kind hosts, then departed White Rock cycling on Marine Drive with a huge vista of the ocean, including views of Washington State. We crossed Hwy 99 on 8 Avenue then made our way near the Peace Arch border crossing to 0 Avenue. This road is a largely

16

unprotected border, with the US on the south side and Canada on the north. There were possibly some scrutinizing video cameras mounted on power poles along the road. We followed 0 Avenue as far as Hwy 11, which would bring us to Abbotsford. We had thought we would be able to eat at restaurants or truck stops along the way, however, this was rural Fraser Valley country, not at all what drivers along the Trans-Canada Highway (TC Hwy) see or what we expected and there were no restaurants in sight. While we were snacking on our GORP (good old raisins and peanuts) at the edge of the road, we met Bob and Joan, a couple from Kamloops who were cycling this section of Canada before cycling the rest of the way across the country. We discussed routes and schedules and found out that Joan still had to teach until the end of the school year before retiring. They would finish the rest of their cycle tour in the summer. We wished them luck on their journey, saying maybe we would meet again. We finally found a truck stop on Vye Road, stopped and asked the attendant for directions and then snaked our way north and east following the Cascade Mountains while staying in the mainly flat valley. We could see Vedder Mountain and came to Vedder Mountain Road, which we cycled along until we could follow signs to the town of Cultus Lake. There were plenty of cars and patrons in the town, even in early May. The drizzle kept the air cool as we set up our tents. After setting up our campsite, we cycled 6 km back and forth to the town for some hot dinner. The park is luxurious (for a BC provincial park) with many campsites and hot showers, albeit in an unheated building. Apparently, in Chinook language, Cultus means "useless," though Cultus Lake is a recreationist's paradise, with plenty of activities like fishing, boating and swimming. The sky was grey and cloudy, but the lake still looked enticingly beautiful.

Day 3, Saturday, May 3
Distance: 81 km to Hope, BC; steady climb out of the valley

As the cafe in town was closed for breakfast, Jen and I said goodbye to Leah outside in the rain as she headed back to Victoria to work. The major hill leaving Cultus Lake was tough to climb but had looked scarier cycling down. Our breakfast stop was at Vedder Crossing. As we left the restaurant, I noticed my first flat tire of the trip. We repaired the flat by cleaning out the tire and replacing the tube. A nearby bike shop, Jack's, let us use their pump and we chatted about cycle touring as I bought another tube and valve covers.

From Vedder Crossing, we cycled north along Vedder Road until we merged onto the TC Hwy. A wide shoulder makes the highway, with all its busy traffic, safe to cycle along. We stopped at Bridal Falls for a short break from the cycling. As we were stretching, a longhaired fellow approached. He was a sales rep for a cycling tool company and he gave us a free sample of his mini tire patch kit—very friendly of him. We easily reached Hope in the mid afternoon, as the sun was just starting to shine. Stopping at the Tourist Information Centre (TIC), we picked up maps and information and took our photos at the Rambo cardboard cutout. They had filmed the Rambo movie, *First Blood*, in Hope in 1982. Our bicycles were covered in road grime from cycling in the drizzle. We asked at a nearby car wash and they let us hose off our bikes.

We cycled through town and met various groups of folks who were also cycling across Canada. Hope seems to be a "Mecca" for cross-country cyclists, as they all have to pass through this crossroads. Each bunch of cyclists has their own schedule, agenda and route. While I waited for Jen outside the grocery store, I met a group of three that were planning on cycling the Coquihalla Highway route (#5). That route always seemed steep even when driving in my old Subaru car, so I wished them luck. As we were cycling to find a restaurant, a pickup truck stopped and the driver flagged us down. We wondered if this was someone we knew. It turned out to be a Swiss fellow who had been on an exchange program in Canada and now was going to cycle across the country on a very zigzag route. We chatted briefly and went our separate ways dubbing him Swiss Alex.

At Kimchi's we ate some great Asian noodles, then started cycling again after 6:00 pm. Upon departure, my front tire was flat AGAIN, so another repair had to be made. I tried to put on the spare tire but it was a Schwalbe Marathon, very stiff and too difficult for us to mount. Most tire or repair shops were closed due to the late hour. Jen found the rock bit causing the leak and removed it. We taped the hole and filled up with air at the gas station, hoping it would suffice and the pressure would be maintained. (Fortunately it held until Winnipeg.)

By the time we got cycling again out of Hope, it was past 7:30 pm and becoming dusk. We found it a bit disconcerting that it was getting darker and the provincial park that was supposed to be 7 km out of town was nowhere to be seen. Luckily, Jen spotted an area beside Hwy 3 that had been logged (a cutblock for foresters reading this) so we decided to camp there before it got totally dark. We hauled our bikes and gear across a ditch to the logging road. We were relieved to find a somewhat level site on the deactivated road upon which we could camp. We found out later that (BC) provincial parks remove their park sign when closed. Many provincial parks are not open early in the season. It also turns out that cutblocks are free, very private and may even have a source of running water. How appropriate for two foresters to be camping in a cutblock on Day 3! It was certainly all part of the adventure and we were able to enjoy the experience.

Day 4, Sunday, May 4
Distance: 60 km to Manning Park; almost all uphill

Lesson Learned: take many short breaks while on a long uphill climb. Jen's Tip: keep looking at eye level instead of up because it helps to be able to see the progress you're making.

In the morning, the stove would not stay lit so we opted for a cold breakfast. We were able to view the cutblock (in the daylight) and walked up the old logging road to find water for cleaning up. Our little tents were dwarfed in the emptiness of the block, surrounded by logging debris and neighbouring coastal Douglas fir trees. We took photos of the cutblock campsite for later identification. The first hill was 8 km of 7% slope! That was a typical uphill challenge on this day full of uphill legs. Before this day, we usually stopped for rest breaks at the top of a hill. We were delighted to realize that we were able to stop for breaks anywhere on the hill and still be able to get moving again. Many short breaks while ascending were advantageous, giving our muscles some much-needed rest. Our first crash occurred today—yikes! Jen was distracted by something, hit the road barrier wall and couldn't remove her shoe from the clip fast enough, falling over on her bike towards the traffic. Thank goodness there was not a lot of traffic and the only resulting injury was a scraped left leg. The strange part was that I was far enough behind her that I did not even witness it!

We reached our first mountain summit sign, Allison Pass Summit, at 1342 m. We felt somewhat triumphant, taking photos of each other at the sign. According to websites, this pass rises 1282 m in 59.1 km (little did we know!). The temperature was about 20°C—balmy! We were into shorts and no jacket for the first time on the trip, yet there was still snow in the forest. When there was a break in the trees, we could see snow capped mountains in the distance as we were cycling on our own steep hill.

When we got to Manning Park Lodge, we encountered a minor dilemma. The front desk staff told us there was no camping possible in the park as the campsites were still snowed out. We asked if we could camp just outside the lodge where there was a nearby grassy area, but our request was denied. We met up with Swiss Alex and as we ate with him in the lodge restaurant, we decided to rent a room together to save money. We were glad to make use of the lodge facilities: nice warm showers, laundry facilities and a large comfortable community lounge. Later in the evening, I managed to find the vertical profiles of the day's leg mixed in with the paperwork and maps—it looked daunting on paper. Knowing that we had completed this stretch from Hope to Manning Park through the Cascades was a confidence booster.

Day 5, Monday, May 5
Distance: 72 km, mainly downhill to Princeton, BC; 90.7 km on the cycle computer (due to a return trip to town)

After a carb-loaded breakfast of pancakes, we got our bikes out from the locker, took photos of the lodge and headed back on the road, joined by Swiss Alex. The road was built along the path of least resistance through beautiful forested mountain scenery. Thankfully, this wilderness is preserved in the provincial park. In the two days we had been travelling through Manning Park, the forest had transitioned dramatically from wet coastal rainforest to dry interior ponderosa pine forest. We took lots of breaks for water, photos and rests after the long climbs through the Cascade Mountains.

There was an enormous downhill where the highway descends 275 m in 3.9 km from Sunday Summit near Copper Mountain. We were braking pretty much all the way down but still getting up to speeds of 50-60 kph! (yikes!). Advice: wear layers of clothing and keep extra clothing accessible. Swiss Alex had removable sleeves and pant legs that he would add or remove as necessary. At some point along this stretch of the road, we lost Swiss Alex as he set forth in a different direction.

> Lesson Learned: don't get your hopes raised; expect disappointing store closures in small towns, i.e. your "Day 5" could be somebody's day off.

We reached Princeton by midafternoon and tried to get information at the TIC. We decided not to travel the Trans-Canada Trail/Kettle Valley route as it was described as 40 km of gravel road. This wouldn't have been easy on our road bikes. We were disappointed to find the bike shop was closed. We did manage to pump air into our tires (even the patched one) at a local auto repair shop. Just outside of town was the Princeton Castle Resort, a gem of a resort with log cabins, a lodge and camping, where we decided to stay for the night. We toured around the remains of an old cement plant, which appear as castle ruins. The mountain pine beetle has affected most pine trees in British Columbia causing huge areas of dead and dying trees. When we set up our tents amidst the dying pine trees, we hoped the wind would not blow them over in the night. We cycled the 5 km into town for a Greek dinner then cycled back to the campsite for showers and a good night's sleep.

Day 6, Tuesday, May 6
Distance: 97 km to Keremeos, BC on Hwy 3 then northeast on Hwy 3A to Twin Lakes Golf Resort

The ride into town for breakfast was as expected, but the next 66 km, mostly downhill from Princeton, was a welcome surprise. The road meandered alongside the Similkameen River ending near Keremeos surrounded by fields of apples, apricots, grapevines, berries and other crops. We had a few short breaks for photos and GORP and reached Keremeos in about four hours—quite speedy. We had a snack break by the fruit stands which unfortunately were not fruit filled in early May. There are so many competing fruit stands in Keremeos that in July, when they are full of fruit, it is fruit heaven.

There was still a lot of daylight left and we were not spent yet so we decided to keep cycling along Hwy 3A towards Penticton. The ride was a 16 km climb to the Twin Lakes Golf Resort, a tough slog at the end of the day. When we talked to the resort owners, they were contemplating disallowing tenters in their campground. Lucky for us, the man asked his wife if we could camp there and she said, "No problem." We set up amidst a few RVs, surrounded by towering rock bluffs and lush green interior fir forests. Fortunately again, the restaurant at the resort was open and we had an excellent meal while enjoying the view over the golf course. A meeting of the local Volunteer Firefighters Society was being held there so we were quite entertained as we ate.

Day 7, Wednesday, May 7
Distance: 33 km to Penticton, BC and rest day

We enjoyed an easy 33 km mostly downhill ride from the golf resort to Penticton, where we had a relaxing rest day. We cycled to Jen's friend Nicola's place, which was at the top of a huge hill. After chatting over breakfast at Nicola's, we headed to the Bike Barn, a local bike shop that Jen had previously dealt with. We bought small parts, pumped air into our tires and chatted with staff about our cycling questions. Penticton has many outdoor enthusiasts and annually hosts a major triathlon in July. Back at Nicola's, we got caught up on laundry, email and the blog and played with baby Olivia. We were thrilled to have a rest day in the sunny Okanagan and sleep in real beds. Nicola's partner, Aaron, advised us to cycle along the side agricultural roads towards Osoyoos, instead of the highway.

Day 8, Thursday, May 8 (Naomi's 16th birthday)
Distance: 72 km to Osoyoos, BC; 81.56 on the computer (due to a return trip to town)

Cycling along the backcountry roads was very pleasant, as we passed at least twenty vineyards or wineries, i.e. Burrowing Owl, Blasted Church, Le Vieux Pin. We passed field after field of picturesque vineyards and blossoming apple orchards with a background of snow-capped mountains. No wonder there are many cyclists and cycle shops in the Okanagan valley. We cycled along the east side of Skaha Lake then down Maple Road to Vaseux Lake, where we stopped for a snack break at the provincial park. As we continued on our way south, the landscape was getting drier and drier, but ironically a big black cloud appeared over us. With little warning, we were in the midst of a massive downpour and suddenly we were getting peppered with small hailstones! We stopped and quickly donned our raingear. We then had to remove it as the rain stopped abruptly and we heated up again. We cycled past Tuc-el-Nuit Lake, down peaceful Black Sage Road to No. 22 Road and then finally back to Hwy 99 South. We were so pleased to have taken Aaron's advice to follow this quieter alternate route for most of the way instead of the busy highway.

At Osoyoos, we stopped at a large, recently built TIC with designs on the wooden floors, filled with wooden structural elements and displays of BC artifacts. Osoyoos is considered a desert town and its elevation is the lowest in the southern Okanagan. With new maps and advice, we cycled to Haynes Point Provincial Park, jutting out into Osoyoos Lake— very scenic. We set up our tents and then the wind changed 180°. We moved campsites to get on the leeward side of the point

> Lesson Learned: ask the local people for advice on where to eat.

again. We cycled into Osoyoos and had an excellent meal at Campo Marina Italian Restaurant which was recommended by the camp attendant. He was so confident we would enjoy our meal that he said he would buy it if we were not satisfied. After eating, we cycled back to camp and I phoned (daughter) Naomi for her 16th birthday. She was in the midst of her birthday dinner at a restaurant.

Day 9, Friday, May 9
Distance: 74.5 km from Osoyoos, BC to Midway, through the 1233 m Anarchist Pass

Jen & I on the Anarchist Mtn Pass; Day 9

While eating breakfast at the ABC Country Restaurant in Osoyoos, we met and chatted with two (relatively) older Swiss-Canadian fellows cycling in the same direction. After cycling uphill for about 15 km, we met them again at the rest area/viewpoint. They had cycled many areas in British Columbia and were familiar with the Crowsnest highway route. Their perspective was to take

Climbing from Osoyoos towards the Anarchist Mountain pass; Day 9 (photo: J. Erlendson)

annual cycling trips while keeping their spouses happy with other trips. We had photos taken with the view behind us and then passed the guys. The view of Osoyoos Lake was stunning and we could still see the point where we had camped the previous night. The town was surrounded by unique arid "desert" plants and animals found nowhere else in Canada. After passing some new land development with statues of a grizzly bear, Sasquatch, eagle, moose, etc., we finally reached the Anarchist Summit of 1233 m ascending 955 m in 30.1 km. We had heard a lot about the difficulty of this summit, so it gave us confidence that we had successfully ascended this mountain pass without enormous hardship. Jen and I kept plodding along, taking breaks when we needed to and finally reached the top. The decision to stay overnight in Osoyoos and tackle the climb to the summit first thing in the morning was a sound one.

From the summit to the next town of Rock Creek was a downhill ride and we arrived to find that only a few shops were open. From Osoyoos to Rock Creek was only about 56 km and there were not a lot of accommodation options in Rock Creek so we decided to keep cycling to the next town of

Midway. This town was so named for the midway point of the railway between the Rockies and the Pacific Ocean.

We reached Midway and were glad to find a campsite beautifully situated on the river. We set up camp and then walked into town to get some groceries and look around. At the grocery store, there was a poster advertising a roast beef dinner and fashion show put on for and by the high school graduates for that very evening. We tried to get tickets at the store, but they recommended going straight to the event as it was sold out and was starting in a half hour. We talked to the lady selling tickets and she was able to find us two: $12 each for an all-you-can-eat buffet dinner. Walking in as a Japanese-Canadian, I noted many local Japanese-Canadians in attendance—likely a legacy of the wartime evacuation from the coast. It would have been interesting for me to go and talk to them, but the opportunity did not arise. Jen and I, on the other hand, likely stood out as the only non-locals attending this local event. The dinner was excellent and the fashion show alone was worth the price of admission. Some of the gowns were vintage from the grads' own grandparents and some were current prom dresses on loan from a store in Kelowna. The few guys who were graduating were not left out. They vied for the title of Ms BCSS (Boundary Central Secondary School). They dressed up as females and competed in bathing suit, talent, formal wear (with heels) contests—a very entertaining show with a mixture of talent, humour, music and speaking. After the end of the show, we were able to easily walk back to the campsite.

Day 10, Saturday, May 10
Distance: 82.72 km and major elevation changes from Midway to Christina Pines campground

Grenburn Coffee provided very tasty French toast for a reasonable price. Lots of locals chatted with us giving us cycling advice. We cycled to Greenwood, where I wanted to get some photos to give to my mom's Japanese-Canadian friend who had been "resettled" to Greenwood during the World War II evacuation. I stopped at the local museum to get some postcards for her as well. We kept climbing (mostly) towards Eholt summit, about 1028 m and then it was mainly downhill, especially the final run into Grand Forks. Just past the entrance to the town was a bike shop, Chain Reaction, where we stopped to browse and pump air into our tires. A fundraiser garage sale was being held in the parking lot, so there were a lot of folks milling about. We chatted about Grand Forks (one of the oldest European settlements in BC), restaurants, cycling routes and the weather, which we heard was about a month behind the norm. We hurried off to the Grand Forks Hotel, where the perogies had been recommended, and arrived just before the rain started in earnest. Again, it paid to listen to the locals for food recommendations. We ate very yummy home-made perogies, pyrahi, and bumbleberry pie, to taste the local Doukhobor food.

The rain eased as we cycled the hilly 20 km stretch to Christina Lake, passing interior fir forests to reach this small tourist town. As it was low tourist season in this summer resort town, shops, restaurants and the provincial park was not yet open for the season. We chose to stay at Christina Pines, a private campground beside the high school. They let us lock our bicycles in their shed for security. The owners recommended an excellent pizza shop facing the highway that we were glad was still open.

Day 11, Sunday, May 11
Distance: 100.68 km, through the Blueberry Paulson pass, 1535 m; 6.1 hrs in the saddle

We knew it would be a long day. We wanted to get an early start, but the coffee shop service in Christina Lake was very slow. We finally got away, unaware that we were to climb uphill for the next 30 km from the lake. Cycling some steep grades of 7-9% was a long slow haul. We just kept our legs pumping which continued to keep our bodies warm. As we kept cycling, we did not realize the high elevation we were at. Our fingers and faces were starting to feel the chill and we were not able to take long breaks, just enough to grab some water or sustenance. We kept wondering when we would reach the summit.

Stopped at the Paulson Bridge, we met a few German cyclists who were scouting the nearby Trans-Canada Trail for a cycle tour they were hoping to lead. The trail in the thickly forested mountains was still

Jen and I at the Paulson Bridge on the pass, 1106 m; Day 11

covered in snow, so they were going to have to postpone their tour or change their route. Snow was piled high in the forests right beside the road. After chatting and getting our photos taken, we were cooling off so we set off again, still in pursuit of the summit.

Another 11 km after the bridge, we reached the Paulson summit at 1535 m, our highest yet! We were actually cycling

through a mountaintop cloud. The elevation was high enough that shortly after 1:30 pm there were great big flakes of snow landing on our jackets. We donned all our winter gear (heavy jacket, better gloves, extra layers, thicker tights, boot covers) and wondered if we should hitchhike down the mountain. Jen was more worried about a maniac driver who might pick us up than about cycling in the snow. The snow changed to rain as we descended towards Castlegar. The downhill after the summit was a crazy 30 km of very steep (again 7-9%) grade into town. For much of about 20 km, we were speeding faster than 40 kph, our fingers and toes becoming more numb by the

Flakes of snow on the descent towards Castlegar; Day 11

minute. As a result of our fingers not working too well, we were barely able to brake and hang on to our handlebars and hoped we would not crash! Luckily, there was not a lot of traffic, but it felt like we were descending a bit too fast. We stopped at the first place possible, a truck stop near the town. Jen had become fairly numb in most extremities and any exposed skin (face). I advised her to take shelter inside the restaurant, where she quickly wolfed down some soup to warm up, while I waited outside to stretch in the now-materializing sun.

To get to my friend Sheri's home, we cycled a final 25 km, which included one final very steep ride—whew! Having a warm home to reach is good incentive to keep cycling. Sheri had been my partner in a summer job when we were at university together and I'd seen her most recently in the spring. We got to Sheri's fairly late but were able to enjoy hot showers, an excellent meal and catching up on stories over the evening. She and I both had different memories of that summer working in northwestern Ontario in the logged areas of the Great Lakes Forestry Company.

Day 12, Monday, May 12
Distance: 88 km through Nelson to Kootenay Lake Provincial Park, along Hwy 3A

We enjoyed breakfast with our hosts, Sheri, Leon and Jenni, before Sheri headed off to work in Nelson, and we walked Jenni to the school bus stop. We felt so very fortunate to have stayed with friends in the Slocan Valley after a long cycling day on Day 11. We then cycled the very pleasant 20 km into Nelson, starting near the Slocan River and Crescent Valley and following the Kootenay River into town. There were several bridges crossing the Slocan River, Kootenay River and part of Kootenay Lake. This valley is home to some of the most picturesque scenery in the province, if not the country. Scenes of lake and river water features, views of lovely forested mountains and beautiful wildflowers, Saskatoon berry and other flowering shrubs abound.

In the heritage capital town of Nelson, we parked our bikes in storage at the first bike shop we encountered (quite a rip-off to have to pay $20 total to store our bikes there!) and walked up to Baker Street, the main street of town. Sheri happened to spot us during her lunch break. We lunched with her at the Kootenay Bakery. We took a hostess photo and said a final goodbye to Sheri, then wandered and window-shopped around the town, including Boomtown Sports. Nelson was once considered for the capital city of the province and has hundreds of beautifully-restored, turn-of-the-last-century heritage buildings. Many residents seem to be craftspeople and many locals live an organic, healthy lifestyle. We supplied ourselves with dried foods at the well-stocked Co-op grocery store, got maps at the TIC, retrieved our bikes from the shop and headed back on the road. The ride to Balfour was a very pleasurable, mainly downhill 35 km along the west arm of Kootenay Lake from Nelson. We caught the 4:30 pm ferry from Balfour to Crawford Bay to cross Kootenay Lake, "the longest 'free' ferry ride in the world". The ferry was the same type that is used by BC Ferries to cross from Swartz Bay to Saltspring Island but unbelievably is free! We definitely lucked out with the weather—very sunny! There was still plenty of snow in the mountains even though it was above 10°C in the valley.

After exiting the ferry, there was a steep climb to

Jen in front of Kootenay Lake and the Purcell Mountains;
Day 12

Crawford Bay, where most of the artisan shops were unfortunately closed. The sun was shining and there were very few vehicles. We decided to keep cycling along the east side of Kootenay Lake on Hwy 3A for another 20 km to Lockhart Creek Provincial Park. Our tent site was amidst the pine and fir trees right across from the lake, with few other tenters at the park. Luckily, an Italian restaurant was across the road, right on the lake and still open. We were able to walk along the beach to take some twilight photos with the setting sun, then walked back to eat at the restaurant. Some customers there warned us that they had just seen a cougar in the park. We kept our senses alert to wild animals and fell asleep without incident.

Day 13, Tuesday, May 13
Distance: 62 km from Lockhart Creek Provincial Park to Creston, BC

After a quick cold breakfast at the park, we paid the self-registration fee just before the park warden came along. Then we cycled along Hwy 3A, managing the minor hills that followed the edge of the lake. The lakeside scenery was picturesque with crystal clear Kootenay Lake in the foreground, pine and larch forests right beside us and the snow-covered Purcell Mountains in the background. At one point, we saw a small black bear in the distant woods but were too far away to get a decent photo.

At the south end of the lake, we passed Wynndel and followed a local's recommendation to take Lower Wynndel Road through the agricultural Creston Valley instead of climbing a steep hill into town. We passed vast farms and the Creston Wildlife Management Area. This is a world-class wetland habitat filled with bird life: heron, ducks and red-winged blackbirds, to mention a very few. Arriving in the town of Creston in the early afternoon, we visited the very helpful TIC then lunched at The Other Place which had excellent home cooking. This lunch stop was recommended by Sheri, our Slocan hostess, and others. Stocked up on baked goods and groceries from the local stores, we then cycled another 5 km out of town to Mountain Park Resort. We set up camp under the forest canopy then actually had time to tour around "off bike". Around the campsite were woodcarvings, e.g. bear faces carved into stumps left from competitions held in previous summers. After a short hike over a bridge, we trekked along some riverside trails, enjoying the chance to wander on foot and to view and photograph spring flowering wildflowers. The Kootenays are certainly some of the most hospitable and charming areas of Canada.

Day 14, Wednesday, May 14
Distance: 102.24 km to Cranbrook, BC

Cycling from the campground through the forested, wide Columbia valley seemed mostly downhill. We stopped at Kitchener, but our hopes for a home-cooked meal were dashed as we saw the CLOSED sign on the restaurant. The next small town we encountered was Yahk, where we ate and talked to the operator about the diminishing employment opportunities there. The original plan was to stay at the provincial park at Moyie Lake, but we changed our minds when we saw how far the campground was from the facilities. All distance becomes relative depending on amenities needed/wanted, hills to climb/descend and many other factors. We decided to press on to the appealing city of Cranbrook, where, with the time zone change (from Pacific to Rocky Mountain time), we arrived into town at about 6 pm. On approaching Cranbrook from the west, we saw our first glimpses of the majestic Rocky Mountains rising up with such grandeur in the distance. What a thrill to see the snow covered rugged peaks and to imagine cycling through a Rocky Mountain pass. Each time I view these amazing geological features, I can only feel awe. The wide valley we were cycling through allowed a wider range of vision of the seemingly untraversable ridges jutting up towards the sky. These mountains may have seemed different than the ranges we had already cycled through as we were able to view them from a distant perspective. The Rockies are visibly craggier buttes, geologically younger looking than other mountain ranges. We felt so tiny in comparison to these gigantic British Columbian and Canadian icons. Yet, we knew that any mountain was passable if ascended in small steps.

Once inside Cranbrook city limits, we passed a closed provincial park and TIC, but at least we found a city map on the TIC wall. We discovered a municipal campground right in the city, so decided to stay there. We used the convenient hot showers and laundry facilities right after we set up our tents. The city is quite pleasant with all the necessary amenities (bike shop, restaurants). Jen and I splurged on our last dinner together eating schnitzel at Heidi's. She contacted her parents who were on their way to meet her at the Best Western, where they stayed that night.

Day 15, Thursday, May 15
Distance: 49.3 km to Jaffray, BC

Yesterday was Jen's last day of cycling so she packed all her gear into her parents' vehicle, then was able to attach her bike and BOB trailer to the bike rack. As I was hoping to be finished with winter weather, I also had Jen's parents take my winter clothes, as well as my camp stove and fuel. We had found it more convenient to buy hot coffee and meals than to buy groceries, cook and wash dishes. After washing up at the Best Western, Jen took us all out for breakfast. Then we had to say our sad goodbyes. As the car departed, I could barely face waving goodbye. I quickly waved, then climbed into the tent to collect my gear and my composure, thinking how difficult it would be to carry on without my friend. Having had the last two weeks of experience with a partner gave me the confidence and determination to carry on with this tour. To start a tour across Canada alone would be very difficult. Cycling across British Columbia gives a cyclist the practical experience of how to manage scheduling, accommodation, food and cycle touring skills that would be useful anywhere.

I went to Gerick Sports Shop for a tire pressure check and another handlebar plug. The cycle computer went a bit spinny, adding on many kilometres before I could stop it. The wireless computer seems to be affected inside bike shops with other computers around. Correct air pressure and shedding possibly 10 pounds of gear (sent back to Victoria with Jen) seemed to make the ride smoother and easier. It seemed a bit strange to be cycling on my own, but I was looking forward to meeting up with my next cycling partner in a few days in Alberta. The spectacular Rocky Mountains are looming all around now—unbelievable scenery. The mountains are massive and so dramatic with their rocky, pointed, snow-capped peaks. The contrast of the Rockies against the blue sky is picture-perfect. This was still Kootenay country, although the landscape/vegetation was transitioning rapidly to high-elevation species. As the elevation increased and cycling became mostly uphill, the temperature also seemed to increase. I made it about halfway to Fernie and decided to camp at Jaffray. The price was right, but the campground was for RVs (recreational vehicles) and not tents. A few of the RV campers were friendly and curious about my tour. The tents had to be set up very far away from the facilities, and later I discovered these sites were closest to the railroad tracks. The golf course adjoining the campground had an air-conditioned dining room. I cooled off while eating there, watching the NHL hockey game, journaling and using my handheld blackberry for blogging. To alleviate safety concerns from family and friends, I carried a blackberry device. Every evening when I was alone, I was to phone home so my family knew my whereabouts and knew that I was safe.

Day 16, Friday, May 16
Distance: 88.96 km Hwy 3 to Sparwood, BC

After about the third time waking up due to a passing train, I decided to get an early start. This was the first day of the May long weekend, seemingly the first weekend for people to go camping. Most of the heavy RV traffic was coming east out of Alberta into BC. The vehicular traffic from BC was possibly a bit heavier than usual and annoying rumble strips were embedded on the highway shoulder. Rumble strips are indented or raised patterns along the edge of the shoulder meant to vibrate to alert drivers that they are leaving the lane. They are the bane of cyclists, unsafe and uncomfortable. When you cross them, the whole bike shudders, making nuts, bolts and cyclists' teeth and brains rattle.

The scenery was outstanding in every direction. I was trying to take photos, but even panoramic shots would not encompass the entire vista of the Rocky Mountains. When cycling through the pass, I tried to imagine how the first settlers and explorers traveled through these very steep mountain passes with little more than a sheep trail. The very tallest peaks were craggy, snow-capped bluffs while lower ridges were covered in high-elevation alpine forest. I stopped at one point to take photos and noticed four nervous young mountain sheep beside the road. There were no adults around and they were a little unsure of what to do. They chose to cross the highway right in front of me and I was lucky enough to get some decent photos of them as they made their way along the craggy bluffs, amazingly camouflaged there.

The weather was perfect for the start of a long weekend but getting too warm for me, about 22°C by early afternoon. I made it to Sparwood, a thriving town with one of the largest coal mines in Canada. There were wonderful facilities in the town, lots of people shopping and a new secondary school. At the TIC, I had my photo taken beside the giant Titan, the largest tandem-axle off-road dump truck in the world, which was used in the local coalmine. After setting up camp at the Mountain Shadows campground, I cycled to the recreation centre to test out the aquatic facilities. How very refreshing to go for a swim in a pool, get the muscles all relaxed and get totally cleaned up. Later I discovered I had lost a pannier bolt so retraced my steps all around town, including the grocery store and aquatic centre. I found it right back at the campground, partially run over but still useable.

> Lesson Learned: the local recreation centre or swimming pool is a great option if no shower facilities exist where you're staying.

British Columbia Cycling

Cycling across BC is not for the faint of heart. With its many steep mountain passes, the cycling is both challenging (climbing the mountains) and invigorating (cruising down the hills). As my home province, I know well there is a great diversity in landscape, vegetation and ecosystems, amazing scenery and plenty of cultural history for the touring cyclist to absorb en route. The roads are (usually) quite bike friendly, especially near the urban centres. The province is full of outdoor enthusiasts and people (in general) are quite used to touring cyclists along the roads. There are many routes for cycling across this province. Most of the roads and some of the trails are outlined with maps and vertical profiles in the Wood book, *Cycling British Columbia*. The Crowsnest Highway (#3) proved to have many climbs, but the steep passes are spread out over the course of the highway. There is much less traffic on this route than the TC Hwy (#1) or the Coquihalla Highway (#5). Having driven through the long tunnels on the TC Hwy and driven the very long steep climbs on the Coquihalla, I was glad I had chosen to travel along the Crowsnest Highway. Cycling across this province first is excellent training for cycling the rest of Canada.

British Columbia Statistics

Distance: 1251.66
Days: 16, including rest day at Penticton
Tent camping nights: 13
Highest elevation: Blueberry Paulson (BP) pass, 1535 m
Largest elevation change in one afternoon: BP pass to
Castlegar: 1535 -433 m = 1102 m

British Columbia

Day	Km	Destination	Route	Notes
1	73	Swartz Bay ferry terminal	Hwy 17 to BC Ferries	rolling hills
		Tsawwassen – White Rock	Hwy 99A s to Exit 10	oceanside
2	87	Cultus Lake Prov Park	Marine Drive, White Rock	oceanside
			8 Ave., 0 Ave., Hwy 11, Vye Rd., Vedder Mountain Rd	rolling farmland
3	81	Hope	Vedder Rd, Hwy 1 (TC Hwy), Hwy 3	Fraser Valley
4	60	Manning Prov Park	Hwy 3, Crowsnest Hwy east	steep mountains
5	90.7	Princeton	Hwy 3, Crowsnest Hwy east	steep mountains
6	97	Keremeos, Twin Lakes	Hwy 3 to Keremeos, Hwy 3A to Twin Lakes	river valley, mountain
7	33	Penticton	Hwy 3A to Penticton	mountain to town, rest day
8	81.56	Osoyoos	Lakeside Rd., east of Skaha Lake, Hwy 97 to Osoyoos	Lakeside
9	74.5	Midway	Hwy 3, Crowsnest Hwy east	Anarchist Mtn pass
10	82.72	Christina Lake	Hwy 3, Crowsnest Hwy east	mountains
11	100.68	Slocan Valley	Hwy 3, Hwy 3A thru Castlegar	Blueberry Paulson Mtn pass
12	88	Kootenay Lake Prov Park	Hwy 3A thru Nelson	along Kootenay Lake
13	62	Creston	Hwy 3A	lakeside and valley
14	102.24	Cranbrook	Hwy 3, Crowsnest Hwy east	valley
15	49.3	Jaffray	Hwy 3, Crowsnest Hwy east	Rocky Mountains
16	88.96	Sparwood	Hwy 3, Crowsnest Hwy east	Rocky Mountains
	1251.7	British Columbia total km		

British Columbia

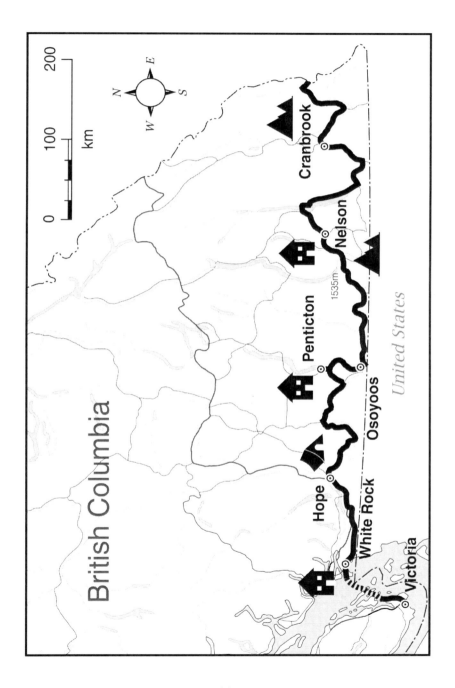

41

British Columbia

Chapter 3
Across the Prairies

Day 17, Saturday, May 17
Distance: 64.28 km to Lundbreck; through the Crowsnest Pass into Alberta

As the temperature was due to warm up again and I had an appointment scheduled, I got an early start. A sign in Sparwood said the temperature was 6°C, but I quickly warmed up and started de-layering. This was the day to cross the border from BC to Alberta and travel through the Crowsnest mountain pass. It did not feel very steep or high and it surprised me when I reached the Crowsnest picnic site/rest area. This was the border of the two provinces, the Continental Divide. I looked back and took a photo of the "Welcome to BC" sign. Just beyond, I passed the site where four rail cars had derailed the previous day. The highway traffic slowed down due to the extra vehicles and allowed me to get a good look at the accident scene. The railway track was quite close to the side of the highway and the rail inspectors' vehicles were on the highway shoulder. The inspectors appeared to be investigating the site. The four derailed freight cars were sprawled off the tracks. The investigation was likely to determine the cause of the derailment as well as to check for spilled loads.

Just into Alberta right beside the highway was a most expansive TIC with an awesome view of the Rocky Mountains, very clean facilities and friendly staff. One staff member took my photo with the mountains that I had just climbed through in the background. I gathered information and maps then continued cycling. A huge tailwind rushing

down from the mountains and the downhill travel made for speedy cruising. The highway had huge debris-free shoulders and even a sign warning drivers to watch for cyclists. At the first town I encountered, Coleman, I stopped for a Kicking Horse coffee and food. I met and chatted with a couple of locals who

Just east of the Crowsnest Pass at the first Alberta TIC, with the Rockies looming behind me; Day 17

had just cycled to Sparwood and back for recreation. While cycling on the highway, two mountain bikers caught up to me, curious about my tour. They offered me accommodation at their nearby cabin in case the provincial park at Lundbreck was full. It's interesting how cyclists chat very easily to one another, even while cycling on the road.

Already, the Rocky Mountains were getting smaller behind me. The valley had widened and become ranch country. The massive Frank slide site surrounded the highway and I took some photos and read the memorabilia. I reached

Lundbreck Provincial Park, the place to meet my husband Peter's parents and my friend Barb (my next cycling partner), but I was early. There was no cell coverage in the valley so I was walking up the hill to try again when I saw their van as they drove into the park. Barb was able to drive Milton and Hope (my parents-in-law) from Calgary in their van so they were all able to meet me in Lundbreck. We were excited to meet according to plan and what a delight to see them all again.

We unloaded Barb's gear and bike and set up our tents at our chosen site. Due to the long weekend, the campground was packed with campers, but we managed to get waterfront property, alongside the river. Barb suggested that Milton and Hope spend the night at a motel in Pincher Creek and we could all eat together there. We drove into the small farming town of Pincher Creek to look around and they booked into a room at the Super 8 motel. I luxuriated in the hot shower of the motel and in the air-conditioned restaurant, while outside temperatures were hovering around 30°C. With plenty to talk about, the meal took a while. Then Barb and I were driven back to the campground, and we said our goodbyes to Milton and Hope. We fell asleep listening to the soothing water sounds of Lundbreck Falls and river.

Day 18, Sunday, May 18
Distance: 123.57 km to Lethbridge, AB; quite a long ride for Barb's first day!

After a quick walk to see Lundbreck Falls, Barb and I started off early to beat the heat of the day. Barb certainly brought good Alberta luck. Three hours of downhill with a tailwind and not too hot was certainly fortunate. The final views of the Rocky Mountains were beautiful with wind generators lined up in the foreground and ranges of snow capped mountains in the background. The mountains were quickly disappearing into foothills. I attempted to take a panorama photo, but it was difficult to capture the beauty of this expansive scene. We were lucky to have the winds at our backs in this VERY windy area. We reached Fort MacLeod and stopped at MacLeod Restaurant for food and water. The weather got hotter and sunnier and the winds played around somewhat after our stop, but we kept going, making the decision to push on to Lethbridge where Barb had friends,

Wind generators in the Rocky Mountain foothills of Alberta; Day 18

Karen and Terry. Cycling through Lethbridge city got a bit hairy, but we finally made it to the Greenhaven Greenhouses, just east of town, which Karen co-owns and manages. Karen fed us, then took us on a private after-hours tour of the largest nursery and garden centre in Lethbridge on their busiest weekend of the year. There were many very modern greenhouses with the latest features, full to the brim with thriving flowers, seedlings, shrubs and trees ready for sale. What a well-run seedling and retail operation. We were so happy we made the decision to reach Karen and Terry's, as we were given such wonderful hospitality!

Day 19, Monday, May 19, Victoria Day holiday
Distance: 76 km to Grassy Lake, AB along Hwy 3

We had a slow start to the day as we said goodbye to our hosts while lingering over breakfast and coffee. Then we were back on Hwy 3 again, with the mountain ranges just a sliver on the horizon, almost out of sight. The landscape was generally quite flat with a few rolling hills. We had a brunch break at Taber, the famous potato growing centre, and took photos beside the potato statue alongside the highway. We also shopped for groceries, in case there were no stores open later due to the holiday. The traffic was light for the holiday Monday. By late afternoon, we reached Grassy Lake, "Home of the Sturgeon Spawning Grounds" (the sign said) which had a campground and was about halfway from Lethbridge to Medicine Hat.

Barb near Grassy Lake, AB; Day 19

Grassy Lake doesn't have many retail shops, but we could walk to a store and buy snacks and beer—how Canadian! The campground was small and deserted with maybe just one other filled campsite. We had plenty of space to stretch and later walked around to take photos of the grain elevators. We were happy to have a place to camp with tap water and washrooms.

Day 20, Tuesday, May 20
Distance: 91.25 km along Hwy 3 to Medicine Hat

We had a great opportunity to study irrigation systems as we cycled along Hwy 3 among the fields of crops: beans, beets, potatoes, grain and corn. We saw a few llama and bison farms and many grain elevators along the rail line, quite close to Hwy. 3. We stopped at the small town of Bow Island and got some fresh fruit, veggies and a sub sandwich for lunch at the IGA store. The wind was getting stronger and there wasn't much shelter. We ended up eating our lunch in the wind shadow of a tree in a farmer's field. The wind increased in strength, becoming a nice tailwind as the road veered to a favourable direction.

We easily reached Medicine Hat, the Gas Capital of Alberta and followed signs to campgrounds near the western end of town. The first campground seemed full of unsavoury residents, shouting obscenities at the manager and asking what he was going to do about all the drug dealers living there. We left that site, followed signs and found the municipal Gas Campground, close by and much more hospitable. This was Barb's last day so she called her husband, Derek, to arrange a meeting spot. We met at the campground and packed Barb's gear and bicycle into their vehicle. All three of us went to the Husky truck stop to eat (quickly) so Derek could drive Barb the long three hour drive back home to Calgary. It was enjoyable to chat with Derek and tough to say goodbye to another good cycling mate.

Alberta Cycling

Cycling from west to east certainly seems to be the best choice since the prevailing wind is usually from the west and the Rocky Mountains. There are lots of cyclists, especially mountain bikers in and near the mountains. The highways with their wide shoulders are well maintained and in good shape for cycling. There are various routes to travel across Alberta. If you look at a road map of the province, the most direct and shortest route appears to be Hwy 3 in the south of Alberta.

Alberta Statistics

Distance: 355.1 km

Days: 4

Tent camping nights: 3

Alberta

Day	Km	Destination	Route	Notes
17	64.28	Lundbreck Prov Park	Hwy 3, Crowsnest Hwy east	Crowsnest pass
18	123.6	Lethbridge	Hwy 3, Crowsnest Hwy east	foothills
19	76	Grassy Lake	Hwy 3, Crowsnest Hwy east	prairie
20	91.25	Medicine Hat	Hwy 3, Crowsnest Hwy east	prairie
	355.1	Alberta total km		

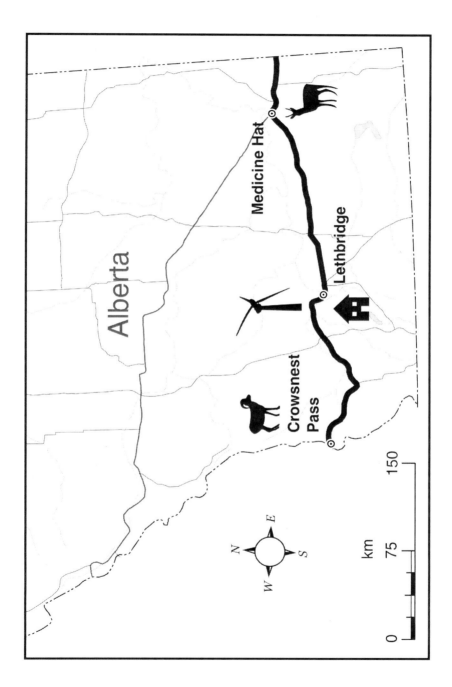

Day 21, Wednesday, May 21
Distance: 103.15 km along TC Hwy 1 to Maple Creek, SK

Suddenly woken up at 4:00 am by a splat, splat, splat sound, I became aware that it was the sprinkler system starting up. The sound was different than the steady pitter patter of the rain and water was nearly coming inside the tent. I quickly pulled the tent and gear out of the direct flow of the sprinkler to avoid getting soaked inside the tent. The camp attendant was quite apologetic when I told him in the morning, saying he had told an employee to make sure the sprinklers were turned off in the campground.

I went to the same Husky truck stop where we'd had supper, had a decent breakfast then cycled to the TIC. The tourist centre gave me directions to the nearby Cyclepath bike shop, where they checked my tire pressure and chain stretch and cranked on a few nuts. On my own again, it felt safer to get my bike checked quickly at a bike shop than to do it myself. Later, after a short grocery stop, I was about 5 km out of town when I realized I had a rear flat tire—such an annoyance! As I was still close to town, I thumbed a ride right back to the bike shop. The driver was a kind retiree working for his son as a driver when needed. As the cycle shop knew me already and knew I was touring, Trent immediately started the service, replacing the flat tire with my spare Schwalbe Marathon tire and a new Goo Tube, a tube which is supposed to seal off a puncture right away and alleviate future flat tires. I bought an extra tube and was out of there as soon as he finished the job. What good luck to be able to return to the bike shop where they could complete the repair job right away. Since the mechanics had been able to replace the flat tire with my new, very stiff spare tire, the old tire became my spare.

I headed out again under greying skies and soon crossed paths with Carmel and Gabe, a cycling couple from Toronto. They had flown from Toronto to Vancouver and were also crossing Canada. We saw each other off and on as we took turns taking breaks. Gradually, the rain began and the wind strengthened. I stopped near the Alberta-Saskatchewan border at Walsh, which had an Alberta TIC and a small truck stop, and added more layers for the rain to soak through. At the border, there was no "Welcome to Saskatchewan" sign, so I was unable to take the mandatory photo. Possibly due to the weather, I started to commune with the animals I passed. Each time I passed a herd of cattle, I stared at the cows causing them to stampede alongside or away. Who knows what they were thinking? There were also interesting prairie birds, among them: meadowlarks with their melodious song, red-winged blackbirds, hummingbirds and hawks. After seeing a beautiful "deer" several times, I tried to take a photo of it and find out what it was. According to the locals, this "deer" was a pronghorn antelope, of deer-like size, tan with a white belly and a huge white tail, common to the prairies.

After cycling another 50 km (in the rain) from the provincial border, I reached Maple Creek, known as the original Cowtown. A relatively large and busy private campground, with the first welcome signs I'd seen in Saskatchewan, was a sight for sore eyes. I expected to see the cycling couple and instead saw Swiss Alex checking the weather forecast. He had traveled from the Okanagan north to the TC Hwy, to Banff and then south again to Hwy 3 somewhere near Medicine Hat. He had been resting at Maple Creek waiting for the wind to die down. I had contemplated waiting out the wind, but there was no way of knowing how long the wait would be. As I was quite wet and cooling down, I set up camp in the picnic shelter, ate and journaled in the laundry room while trying to dry my gear.

Day 22, Thursday, May 22
Distance: 85.54 km along TC Hwy 1 to Swift Current, SK

I left about 9:00 am heading to the TIC, where the staff were very friendly and helpful. The wind strengthened to a brutal east headwind of about 40 to 60 kph. I never expected to go only 10 kph and into granny gears in the middle of the prairies. Unfaltering wind could be more brutal than cycling through mountain passes as there was no letting up, no flying downhill, just continuous, tough slogging. The wonderful granola bars, home-made by Barb, regularly kept me motivated to continue. Every hour or so, I would allow myself a break for a granola bar taste to spread out the treats. I kept leapfrogging with Carmel and Gabe and once I saw Swiss Alex. We were all getting immensely tired of that wind.

Saskatchewan grain elevator; Day 22

In the late afternoon, I was taking a rest stop near Gull Lake with another 50 km to get to my destination and wondering how or if I would reach Swift Current. A fisherman towing a boat on his way to Kenora stopped at the side of the road and asked if I wanted a ride. As my bicycle fit neatly into his boat and a ride to Swift Current only took about an hour, I gladly accepted his offer. I was so grateful to reach Swift Current, as I was able to find my way to Wallace's home. He is a brother of my friend Barbara (from Victoria). He fed me, let me have my own space downstairs and I was able to clean up and make myself at home. As a local, he was able to tour me around in a car showing me the highlights of Swift Current and the federal Forestry Experimental Station. We picked up Wallace's wife, Barbara, from her downtown gift shop and then had tea back at their place. More luxury was being able to use their home computer, Googling, especially the local weather. The forecast was for continued easterly winds, average of 50 kph and gusting to 70 kph—yikes!

Day 23, Friday, May 23
Distance: 91.5 km along TC Hwy 1 to Chaplin, SK; wind and salt fog

After a breakfast of homemade muffins and coffee and saying goodbye to my hosts, Barbara and Wallace, I was off to a late start. I knew that it would be slow progress with the relentless east headwind. The wind was definitely persistent, but I put my head down and kept changing position on my bike. Physically and mentally, this leg of the tour cycling into the headwind was a strain. My body was getting exhausted with the non-stop wind, with no chance for a break. One time, when my body needed a change in position, I even got off my bike to walk, as it seemed I could walk faster than I could cycle. Mentally, there was not a lot to keep my brain occupied. Every time I looked up, the scenery was pretty much the same: fields of flat prairie landscape growing grains, wide-open skies, roads that led straight ahead and never-ending wind.

My goal for the day was to reach Chaplin, about halfway to Moose Jaw.

Close to Chaplin, there was a terrible salt storm like a fog, just off Reed Lake near Morse. The salt fog was brutal. White salt hung in the air and attached itself to everything: my bike, panniers, chain, glasses, EVERYTHING! At a truck stop, where I stopped for a much-needed break, I asked locals and travelers about the salt phenomenon. It seems the salt (sodium sulphate) is mined at nearby Chaplin and the hurricane-like wind was blowing it all over. There's a huge pile there which looks a lot like snow—an odd scene in the middle of May.

I finally made my goal and reached the campground at Chaplin by about 9:30 pm in the near dark. I was so thankful to find a campground with running water and a washroom. I was able to check in and call home. It was a private campground and as I was the only camper at the site, I was able to stretch to my heart's content. As I stretched, I thanked my lucky stars that I had made it through this very challenging day. One good consequence of travelling alone was that I did not inflict this leg of the trip on a friend. This day would have turned off any non-cyclist enthusiast thinking they were going to have a good time. I washed up as much as I could, curled up in my sleeping bag and contemplated one of the most brutal days of the trip.

Day 24, Saturday, May 24
Distance: 29.83 km along TC Hwy to Moose Jaw, SK

Upon waking and discovering all my gear and bicycle covered in white salt from the previous day, I attempted to clean off as much of it as possible, using paper towels from the campground. Cycling into the humble town of Chaplin, I looked around for somewhere to eat. I was able to find a small shop that sold me a coffee, but nothing else was open. I sat and chatted with the local farmers who were wondering when the next rains would come, lamenting the wind and arid conditions. I was also lamenting the wind, which was unrelenting.

I decided to listen to music on my MP3 player for the first time while cycling on this trip. Music is much easier on the brain to listen to than the howling wind. The day before, at a gas station near Herbert, I had met a couple that felt sorry for me but couldn't offer me a ride at that time. Fortunately for me, that good-hearted couple watched for me and, when they saw me, stopped and offered me a ride to Moose Jaw. I accepted their compassionate offer and easily loaded my bike and gear into their truck. Abe and Agnes owned a llama farm near Salmon Arm, BC and were in Saskatchewan to help move an elderly relative. The drive along the highway took about an hour by truck and would have taken all day by bicycle. My whole being appreciated the good deed by Abe and Agnes. When they dropped me off, it was only about 5 km to the TIC on the other side of town, but it took a good 20 minutes to reach it. Inside the tourist centre, I was fortunate to meet another cyclist, Doug, and his wife, Anna Marie. He was cycling from Alberta to Nova Scotia and she was driving the support van, so Doug could eat and sleep wherever. They generously offered and served me warm soup and sandwiches in their wind-free RV parked beside the TIC. I began a contact list of other cross-country cyclists and kind strangers that I was starting to meet. These kind gestures seemed like favourable omens to continue on this journey of mine. I cycled to the local bike shop, Boh's, for a quick checkup and shopped a bit. The shop kindly let me store my bike inside there so I could tour the town without worrying about theft. I had plenty of time to actually wander around the historic buildings of Moose Jaw, go to a bank and then sit in a coffee shop, drinking coffee and reading the local paper. I also bought some dried fruit and nuts from a very well stocked bulk food store.

I retrieved my bike and cycled to the Riverside campground beside the river. After checking in and setting up, I was able to wash still more of the salt off my gear, after which I was finally able to enjoy a toasty warm shower. While writing my journal, a young Asian-Canadian fellow camper approached, introduced himself and we chatted. He was Daniel, freelance journalist from North Vancouver driving across Canada, writing stories along the way. We were the only tenters at this campground. We decided to splurge and go to Boston Pizza for dinner so we could watch the opening game of the Stanley Cup finals, Detroit vs. Pittsburgh.

Day 25, Sunday, May 25
Distance: 80 km along Hwy 39 to Weyburn, SK

As I cycled out of the campground, I could feel a directional change in the wind, not directly from the east. The highway I decided to travel along was headed southeasterly, which meant the wind was less of a factor this day. Still gusting hard, it was more from the side than head on. As I broke camp, the rain was just drizzling. It got heavier as I cycled the 50 km to Rouleau. The wind must have increased the chill factor, as my gloves were soaked through and my fingers were immobile when I got to the town. My fingers would not work to sign the guest book where they filmed the TV show, *Corner Gas*. I had to get another person to sign for me and take a photo with my camera. I headed into the Pigeon Cafe to warm up with eggs, toast and soup until my fingers started working again. The fellow working there showed me some *Corner Gas* video, so I would have an idea what the town was famous for.

When I had warmed up, I cycled along the road again until I reached an intersection with the road from Regina. Coincidentally, some neighbours from the campground the previous night noticed me and stopped to confer. They asked if I wanted a ride to Weyburn and, after an affirmative nod, loaded my soaking bike and gear into their nice dry camper. As we chatted in the vehicle, they suggested I could stay at their house in Weyburn, rather than camp at the municipal campground. Of course, I couldn't refuse their Saskatchewan hospitality and went home with Jim and Elaine. They made me feel at home, where I had a hot bath, did a load of laundry and enjoyed hot chowder and their friendliness. The Weyburn weather forecast said there was a chance of wet snow and a low of 0°C, so I was very fortunate to be inside a cozy warm home.

Day 26, Monday, May 26
Distance: 117 km along Hwy 13 to Carlyle, SK

Jim had noticed that my front tire was flat, so lucky for me I was in a dry garage to fix it. The spare tube was retrieved and I decided to patch this tire and get a new one in Winnipeg. Jim had an air compressor so I was able to fill the tires with air right there in the garage. My hosts then took me out to breakfast at El Rancho and I had excellent French toast. Elaine had to go to work and Jim toured me around Weyburn where I got some Saskatchewan photos of the Weyburn wheat sheaves sculpture, the Tommy Douglas church and a W.O. Mitchell wall mural.

After the tour, we returned to the garage and the tire repair seemed fine. I packed, took some photos and said a final thank you and goodbye. I put my MP3 player on and settled into cycling mode. As I mulled over my recent encounters with strangers, I realized that a little help from all these strangers gave me fond memories of Saskatchewan to contrast the memories of the brutal wind.

Early in the day, I spotted a resting cyclist reading at the side of the road. I went over to chat and met Bess, a retired (65 year-old?) woman from Nelson, BC, another woman cycling across Canada. She was taking her time, having rest days if the weather was too uncomfortable and had no time frame at all to reach Newfoundland. Her plan was to stay in Newfoundland for the winter, then cycle back to Nelson, BC by the fall of 2009. Meeting her was further inspiration to carry on this adventure of mine. Even though I did not consider quitting, it still was motivating to meet other touring adventurers. How could I quit when there were friends and family booked to meet me along the way for their cycling adventure? I saw Bess once more at a Stoughton truck stop where she was arriving just as I was leaving.

The winds were more reasonable, so I decided to press on to reach the town of Carlyle. There was much more oil industry in this southeastern section of Saskatchewan, as evidenced by many pumps in the fields. The wheat fields looked magnificent as the setting sunlight shone on them. According to my previous hosts, there were many Saskatchewan returnees and new immigrants here.

By the time I reached the Carlyle campground, evening had arrived. There was a sign for campers to use the swimming pool facilities, but all appeared closed. So I set up camp in a corner near some trees in a non-designated campsite.

Saskatchewan Statistics

Distance: 507 km
Days: 6
Tent camping nights: 2 paying, 2 nonpaying
Home accommodation: 2 nights

Saskatchewan

Day	Km	Destination	Route	Notes
21	103.15	Maple Creek	Hwy 1 (TC Hwy)	prairie
22	85.54	Swift Current	Hwy 1 (TC Hwy)	prairie, major wind
23	91.5	Chaplin	Hwy 1 (TC Hwy)	prairie, major wind
24	29.83	Moose Jaw	Hwy 1 (TC Hwy)	major wind, a helpful drive
25	80	Weyburn	Hwy 39	prairie, a helpful drive
26	117	Carlyle	Hwy 13	prairie
	507.02	Saskatchewan total km		

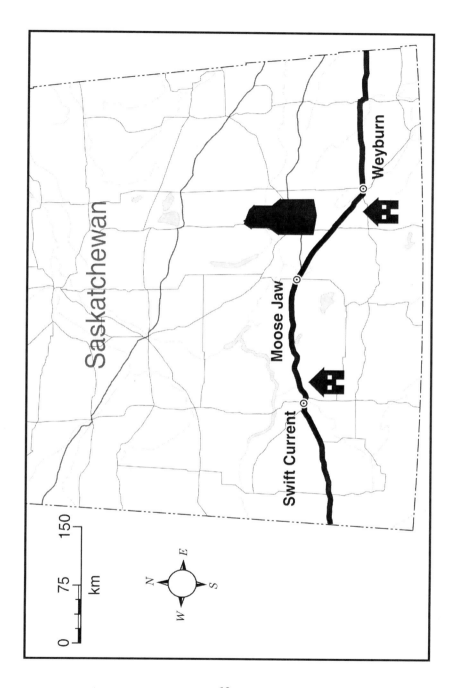

Day 27, Tuesday, May 27
Distance: 91.4 km along Hwy 13 in Saskatchewan which becomes Hwy 2 to Reston, MB

As I packed up camp, park workers were working on a task and thankfully ignoring me. I cycled into nearby Carlyle for coffee and banana bread, and a chat with the locals.

I cycled up and down a few hills to Redvers, on the Redcoat Trail, which followed the route of the Northwest Mounted Police (forerunners of today's Royal Canadian Mounted Police) and had my

> Lesson Learned: campgrounds beside golf courses tend to have more services, including good food.

photo taken with a Redcoat statue outside the town TIC. Crossing the border into Manitoba into the Central time zone, the third time zone so far, I was able to travel at more than 20 kph for the first time on the prairies, as the wind speed had decreased dramatically. The main problem with cycling in Manitoba was the lack of paved shoulders on the highways. So far, all the shoulders seemed to be gravel! I had heard the TC Hwy 1 had gravel shoulders, which was one reason I avoided that route. The golf course in Reston also operated a campground with hot showers and amenities. I set up camp and chatted with some golfers. The evening was very pleasant to wander through the small town on foot, eat at the Creamee and read.

Day 28, Wednesday, May 28
Distance: 72.754 km along Hwy 2 to Souris, MB

The temperature may have dropped down to 0°C that night, but I was cozy enough to sleep well. At the golf course cafe, I drank coffee while watching Canada AM on TV and reading the newspapers. After eating a granola bar, I packed up and headed off. The day was pleasant, about 15-20°C, an east wind but not too strong. The landscape was still quite flat, not as dry and there were definitely increasing numbers of trees and vegetation, acting as windbreaks.

The gravel shoulders on the Manitoba roads are really a problem for both vehicles and cyclists. Not very bike friendly at all!

I cycled into Souris in the early afternoon, giving me enough time to tour the town and campground. It appears to be the only town with more than 1,000 people along Hwy 2. At least I was able to shop in town for fruit, munchies and

sunscreen and had a wonderful lunch. I was disappointed that the library and museum were closed, as I had time to view them. When I went to the famous swinging bridge, a family of German tourists was also visiting. Their children were running the length of the structure to feel it

Souris Swinging Bridge; Day 28

swing. We took each others' photos walking along the bridge, enjoying the company. There was a sign stating that this Souris bridge is "Canada's longest historic suspension bridge built in 1904," apparently 132 feet longer than the Capilano Suspension Bridge spanning Capilano Canyon in North Vancouver. The Souris Bridge certainly has some swing and is absolutely picturesque in a small peaceful prairie town. The Riverside Campground was quite restful.

Day 29, Thursday, May 29
Distance: 92.288 km along Hwy 2 to Spruce Woods Provincial Park, near Glenboro, MB

Lots of quacking ducks and calling peacocks provided a wake-up call at this Riverside Campground. I returned to the cafe where I had eaten the day before and enjoyed an excellent waffle with coffee and yogurt and packed a bagel for lunch. A cafe of this quality in a town of only 2,000 people was impressive to find.

As the forecast was for rain, I put my contact lenses in, but it only showered here and there. Some interesting topographical features meant that I had to change gears for a change. I actually had to coast down into a valley to the Souris River then climb out the opposite side in granny gears. On the whole, more farms, businesses and residences were visible by the roadside than in Saskatchewan. I reached the small town of Glenboro close to 5:00 pm and ate a real dinner of pasta and salad at a local restaurant. The best part was that I was able to log onto their computer to check emails and post my blog. There seemed to be limited cell coverage as the Blackberry was giving me a "data connection refused" message. Without it, I had to look for Internet connections where possible. I was able to email Terri, my sister-in-law and next host and arranged to talk to her on the phone. We were trying to plan a meeting day and place. Glenboro seems to be known for being the gateway to Spruce Grove Provincial Park. As it was not too far off the route, I decided to investigate Manitoba parks. This park was very large and definitely too empty. Perhaps May was too early for the Manitobans to go camping.

Day 30, Friday, May 30
Distance: 85.926 km along Hwy 2 towards Winnipeg, MB

In the middle of the night, a massive thunderstorm suddenly passed over. Counting the seconds between the tremendous thunder and lightning flashes was a bit disconcerting. It went through my head that not many people really knew where I was, though I had left messages at home and with Terri. There seemed to be no employees at the park, just a tree frog and a coyote. I opted to stay cozily snug in my tent as that seemed safer than running out into the lightning amidst all the tall trees to reach the well-lit, concrete washroom centre.

In the morning, I cycled back to Glenboro for eggs and toast. The day was cool and cloudy until the sun broke later in the day—quite enjoyable for cycling. Alongside the highway was a statue of Sara the Glenboro camel, emblematic of Manitoba's only desert (as the sign said). I was about to take a photo of the Sara roadside attraction when I noticed Carmel and Gabe also taking photos there. Meeting them again was a coincidental encounter and we exchanged contact information this time. A little while later, after lunch at Holland, a very dusty car pulled over in front of me. I did not recognize the car. The driver turned out to be Daniel, who recognized me on my loaded bike. He had traveled many more kilometres than I had (via vehicle) and it was another coincidence that he was travelling the same highway at the same time. I gave him a (somewhat heavy) Alberta travel guide book that Barb had given me that I didn't need any more, as he was due to return to the west via car. It amazed me to meet folks crossing Canada, go our separate ways and then coincidentally meet up again.

I had lots of time to reach my next destination so I continued on cycling at quite a leisurely pace. I reached St. Claude around 4:00 pm and took a quick tour around the small predominately French-Canadian town. Unfortunately, the dairy museum was closed. By now, I was used to closed tourist attractions in small towns (especially when I had time to view them!). I found the "meeting place" in town, the Shell restaurant where I was to meet Terri and Pat, my husband's sister and her husband. They had driven from Winnipeg to pick me up and we drove in their truck to their home. This was the first time for me to visit their architect-designed house—quite the designer accommodation! Terri and Pat then drove me, along with Terri's and my bikes, to the Olympia Bike Shop, where the mechanics spent about 45 minutes working on my bike. They rewrapped my handlebar tape, cleaned the Saskatchewan salt off the chain as best they could and searched for the correct size of Schwalbe Marathon tire (which was not in stock). After all this (free) work on my touring bike, Terri asked if they could help her with her bike. As a local, she felt discriminated against when they told her they were booked for another ten days! Pat drove home to start the dinner while Terri and I cycled back across Assiniboine Park to their home. I called home to chat, showered, ate a marvelous home-cooked meal and had lots of space to sleep and sprawl in their TV room. Terri told me she couldn't believe how much I could eat, catching up on some calories!

Day 31 and 32, Saturday, May 31 and Sunday, June 1 rest days in Winnipeg

The days of relaxing downtime were thoroughly enjoyable as I was Terri's assistant with yard work, shopping and buying dried goods at a local Winnipeg health food store.

I cycled across Assiniboine Park to return to the Olympia Bike Shop to get the most puncture-resistant tire in stock installed on my bike. Assiniboine Park is an outstanding urban greenspace, walking distance from Terri and Pat's, full of activity, home of the world's longest skating trail and very handy cycling trails. We ate at Edohei Japanese Restaurant for delicious sushi and appetizers. Six months worth of family stories were related over the course of a couple of days. We watched *Into the Wild* video, gathered fresh rhubarb from their backyard and made a strawberry-rhubarb pie. I caught up on the journal, blog, emails, laundry, mail sent and received. Lazing around with familiar relatives for a couple of days is a good recipe to unwind.

Day 33, Monday, June 2
Distance: 99.675 km to Whiteshell Provincial Park, Brereton Lake campground

After a last, leisurely coffee and breakfast with Terri and Pat, I was packing up getting ready to hit the road again. I was so grateful to them for such an enjoyable couple of days, but it was time to move on. Terri drove me, bike and gear to Anola on Hwy 15, about 23 km east of town—quite a helpful

distance! We said our goodbyes and had a last big hug so she could carry on with her day. I cycled another 52 km to Elma where I stopped for brunch. The route turned north on Hwy 11 then east again onto Hwy 44. Just before Rennie, I met Tim, a newbie touring cyclist. I chatted with him and noted that he was struggling with way too much gear. I

Sign at Whiteshell
Prov. Park, MB;
Day 33

stopped in Rennie for food and directions then headed to Whiteshell Provincial Park campground, another 8 km.

The landscape had changed since Winnipeg from Prairies into Boreal Forest and Canadian Shield country with lots of boggy black spruce/tamarack. The weather was fine—not too windy or sunny, just about 15°C, excellent for shorts and jersey.

Cycling across the Canadian Prairies

In general, the landscape is quite uniformly level and there is plenty of big sky to look at. As there are great distances between towns, the prairies can seem remote. One big factor affecting cycling on the prairies is the wind. The wind can come from any direction and can certainly seem ceaseless, as there are not many trees. The local people are used to the unforgiving weather and are there to help out their neighbours, even touring cyclists. The Manitoba roads are not very bike-friendly with mainly poor gravel shoulders. The most amazing part of the prairies (and maybe all of Canada) is the presence of private, municipal and provincial campgrounds in so many of the towns.

Manitoba Statistics

Distance: 539.31 km
Days: 7, including 2 rest days in Winnipeg
Tent camping nights: 2 paying, 2 nonpaying
Home accommodation: 3 nights at Terri and Pat's

Manitoba

Day	Km	Destination	Route	Notes
27	91.4	Reston	Hwy 13/Hwy 2 in MB	prairie
28	72.75	Souris	Hwy 2	prairie
29	92.29	Spruce Woods Prov Park	Hwy 2	prairie, lightning storm
30	85.93	Winnipeg	Hwy 2	a drive to relatives
31, 32	0			rest days
33	99.68	Whiteshell Prov Park	Hwy 15, 11, 44	prairie transition to boreal
34	97.27	Kenora	Hwy 44/Hwy 17 in ON	boreal forest
	539.3	Manitoba total km		

Manitoba

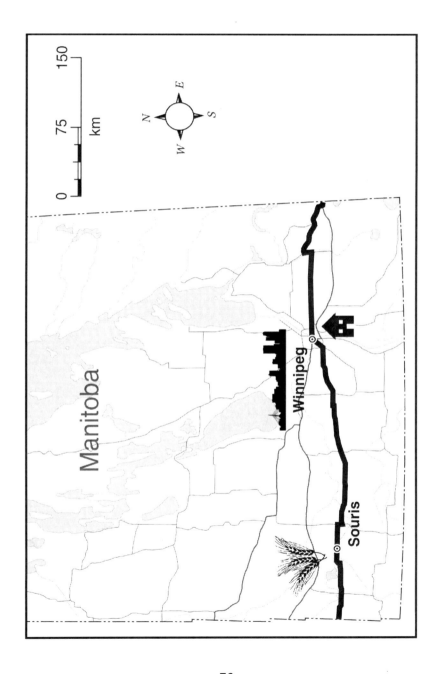

Manitoba

Chapter 4
The Widest Province, Ontario

Day 34, Tuesday, June 3
Distance: 97.267 km along Hwy 44 to Ontario border
then Hwy 17 to Kenora, ON

From the campground, eastbound along Hwy 44, the landscape consisted of many boggy areas, boreal forest, beautiful lakes and small hills. Travelling eastward, the environment seemed to transform from thick forest to cottage country. Increasing signs of civilization were visible as I approached West Hawk Lake where I stopped, had a filling omelet and filled up my water bottles. Seeing trees and lakes again brought real joy to my soul, very much missed on the prairies. Cycling along, I tried to identify the species of mainly tamarack, black spruce, jack pine, white birch and other hardwoods.

Cycling east along Hwy 17, I crossed the border from Manitoba to Ontario and reached Kenora around 4:00 pm. A pleasant cycle through town brought me to the Medical Centre where Peter Harland works. He is the dad of an underwater hockey mate and my next host. (In case you're asking what the heck underwater hockey is, it is hockey played on a pool bottom using mask, snorkel, fins, special hockey sticks and a weighted puck. I have played since university, meeting other players from all across Canada and around the world.) I stopped in to let him know I had arrived and planned to return around 5:15 pm. I cycled into Kenora, a small town with many recreational activities, built all around the Lake of the Woods. I took a requisite photo of the Husky the Muskie monument. For some reason, many small towns across Canada have "Big Things" which are tourist attraction monuments that need to be photographed, commonly with the tourist in the picture. I bought some insect repellent and stopped into the local bike shop, Hard Wear, to check tire air pressure.

A friendly couple waved me down to chat about touring. They were Jeremy and Andrea, about to embark on their own challenging multi-sport adventure: canoeing from Kenora to Thunder Bay, kayaking Lake Superior to Sault Ste. Marie then cycling to the Maritimes. Adventure tourists seem to inspire one another, to find a challenge, to somehow make the logistics work and to actually embark on the trip. I hurried back to the medical centre to meet Dr. Harland.

I loaded my bike into the Harland vehicle; we stopped quickly for groceries then drove to the Harland home. What an ideal location, on Storm Bay, part of Lake of the Woods, about 25 minutes from town. The family all had events that night so I was left to clean up my gear and do my own thing. Again, it was very kind of virtual strangers to let me stay with them and I appreciated the hospitality.

Day 35, Wednesday, June 4;
Distance: 138 km along Hwy 17 to Dryden, ON;
Aaron Provincial Park

I got an early 7:00am start, as my host, Peter, gave me a ride to the highway before heading off to his rowing practice. We said goodbye at the edge of the highway and went our separate ways.

About 60 km after Kenora, it began raining. I waited for a meal break at Vermilion Lake before changing/adding more clothes. I finally figured out that when it rained, my face moisturizer/sunscreen was seeping into my eyes causing stinging. It turns out the TC Hwy along this route had very wide shoulders, agreeable for cycling. It makes the ride much

Moose Danger sign along Hwy 17 in NW Ontario; Day 35

more pleasant when not having to worry about the road surface. As I rode along, there was plenty to observe in the bush. The boreal forest abounded with black spruce bog, including jack pine, tamarack and even white pine trees, many interesting colours and shapes of rock formations and numerous water features. I kept looking for moose as this was prime moose habitat and there were multiple moose warning signs along the highway.

I reached Dryden by about 5:30 pm, just in time to rush into a souvenir shop before it closed. I really wanted to buy some souvenirs with Dryden on them for my son Kai's buddy named Dryden. Luckily, I was able to find some quickly at the Boffo Gift Shop and the TIC. Just outside the TIC, I had my photo taken with the Maximilion the Moose monument, then had a stop at the grocery store and the Timmy's (Tim Horton's) to warm up and dry off. I used the Tim's gift card for the first time as it was Camp Day when all purchases help fund children to attend summer camp. I quickly made a dash for the provincial park before it got dark. I was able to set up camp close to the facilities, and I basked in a hot shower.

Day 36, Thursday, June 5
Distance: 110.24 km along Hwy 17 to Ignace, ON;
Sandbar Lake Provincial Park; moose sighting

The next morning I did some bike maintenance which was required after travelling in rain the previous day. Using paper towels, I wiped down my bike and tire rims and used my trusty lube kit to oil the chain, then tried to dry my gloves and some clothes with the electric hand dryer in the washroom.

The terrain was rolling hills and continuing black spruce bog. From a distance, I thought I saw a man by a roadside swamp and wondered what he was doing. As I got closer, I realized the object was two sizable moose snacking from the bog right beside a large cedar tree. As soon as I stopped to try to take a photo, the moose ran into the bush. It was quite a highlight just to see them, after the numerous Beware of Moose signs! The weather was around 10-15°C, cloudy with slight north winds and fortunately there were not too many bugs.

Forestry still appeared to be the main industry in this area of Ontario between Dryden and Ignace. Cycling along, I was dredging up memories of working in this forested area 30 years ago, during the summer of 1978. My job consisted of driving around with Sheri, who was my host in the Slocan Valley, BC, to various cutblocks and counting regeneration (small seedlings, mostly natural). We got very good at using maps for navigating, a skill that was especially useful on this trip. Our home base was Sheri's home in Thunder Bay and we would drive back there most weekends. There used to be some shops at Borup's Corners, but it seems only ghosts inhabit the town now. Rocky outcrops and more hills were all part of the challenge in this day's ride, giving my legs a good workout. I stopped to eat a real meal at the Ignace truck stop and talk to the locals. Due to some flooding and other reasons, there was a "boil water" advisory for the area where I was heading. This meant buying and carrying extra water, which translated into more weight! This was not a pleasant prospect.

Outside the Ignace TIC, I recognized some PRT seedling boxes filled with red pine seedlings ready for planting. PRT is a seedling nursery company started with employees of the BC Forest Service where I currently work.

I cycled the 11 km from Ignace to Sandbar Lake Provincial Park. This park is 5,000 ha of forest at the southern limits of the boreal forest and Canadian Shield. To keep the black flies away, I sat writing my journal in the wind alongside the clear blue lake.

Day 37, Friday, June 6
Distance: 37.20 km along Hwy 17 to Thunder Bay, ON; flooding and road closures

A giant wind and rainstorm wreaked havoc overnight and continued throughout the morning. I had to wait for a small break in the weather just to pack up. On the 12 km ride back to Ignace, I decided this was a good day to hitch a ride instead of cycle. The "boil water" advisory in the area meant I would have to pack all my water and food in this isolated area of Ontario in very nasty weather. When I went to have breakfast at the Tempo truck stop, I talked to a trucker who had just come from Thunder Bay. He said there was flooding on the highway and it was not safe. That reinforced my decision to catch a ride past the flooding. I stood on the side of the highway right by the truck stop and stuck out my thumb. One trucker came over and said he could pack my bike onto his load, as he was heading to Thunder Bay. I was very thankful, especially when I saw the road conditions as we were driving. Flooding was everywhere beside the highway and the main Hwy 11/17 was closed down heading into Thunder Bay. The alternate route, Hwy 102, was not as wet but very hilly and I was again thankful to be in a truck. The decision to catch a ride instead of cycle that 220 km was soundly based on safety. The driver drove me to a mall close to the airport, where I disembarked the truck and retrieved my own wheels.

On my own again, I stopped at a nearby car rental agency, where they gave me a small map so I could get my bearings. I cycled to the library for Internet access to look at my email and Google. I searched "warm showers" and "couch surfing" websites for accommodation as it was difficult to camp in a major town. Luckily, there was a Mr. Marshall in Thunder Bay, who was a Couch surfing "ambassador" with a phone number contact. His roommate, Aaron, was home and gave me directions to their house. Thanks to another map from the library, I was able to cycle past Lakehead University en route to my newfound accommodation. This lodging was the entire basement suite of an old 3-story house, with lots of space to sprawl and dry out my wet gear. I came upstairs and the friendly folks offered me a beer and an excellent pasta meal. After eating and chatting about travelling, I went out and cycled around town to tour the waterfront. There was plenty happening in town, and a blues festival appeared to be starting. Security and police were surrounding the venue, and I wandered around Thunder Bay on a summery Friday evening. I bought some beer, which was an inexpensive donation to the house in exchange for the deluxe accommodation.

Day 38, Saturday, June 7
Distance: 124 km along Hwy 11/17 towards Red Rock, ON

Terry Fox Memorial, near Thunder Bay, ON; Day 38

I quietly packed up and left a quick note of thank you to the household. It took a while to exit the town, but I finally reached TC Hwy 11/17 with excellent views of Lake Superior and Thunder Bay. I departed the highway to visit the scenic lookout with its wonderful memorial to Terry Fox. His memorials both at the start of this trip (Mile 0 in Victoria) and here at Thunder Bay were inspirational monuments. Thoughts of this young man running across this country on one good leg to raise awareness and funds for cancer filled me with motivation.

This was a pleasant cycling day, and I was able to wear a t-shirt and shorts. There was a tailwind, dome cloud and it was mostly sunny, around 20°C. There was some road construction but, where that was completed, the road and shoulder were in excellent condition, with lots of space and few small hills. I decided I had enough time and legs to take a detour to the Ouimet Canyon. It turned out to be a 25 km round trip on a road

> Lesson Learned: tourist attractions do not always live up to the brochure descriptions; it may not always be worth veering off the main route to see them.

that was WAY TOO STEEP and had a less-than-spectacular view. Expectations were high to see an incredible canyon view, but it definitely was not worth the effort. I cycled the final 25 km to the quaint Birchwood campground near a place called Red Rock. The brochure said, "The place to stop, small but great" — true, with home-cooked meals and organic items for sale right on site.

Day 39, Sunday, June 8
Distance: 118.05 km along Hwy 11/17 to Terrace Bay, ON

The Birchwood was my favourite campground thus far with very friendly hosts, laundry facilities and a cafe right on site. They let me have an hour of free Internet access, so I was able to post another blog item. I had an excellent breakfast of French toast at the Birchwood Cafe, then packed up and started cycling towards Nipigon. There I went to the TIC and got information on the next campgrounds at Terrace Bay and a map of Lake Superior. The map told me that Lake Superior is the largest fresh-water lake in the world by area and holds 10% of the world's surface fresh water. The route following the north shore of Lake Superior was the Trans-Canada Highway. I preferred to stay off the TC Hwy, but there really was not a lot of choice. I took many photo stops along the way with wonderful views of the lake. There was a section with very cool offshore winds, reminiscent of cycling near the ocean and I had to don warmer gear for a short while. Several steep hills for climbing and descending made for interesting cycling. When I reached the town of Schreiber, I recalled stories my dad had told me of this town. During the Second World War, all people of Japanese descent were forced to move from the west coast of Canada, being considered possible security threats. Single men of my dad's age at the time (about 20) were allowed to move out of British Columbia if they went to a road-work camp. He worked at a camp called Jackfish road camp just east of Schreiber and spent his twentieth birthday there. It reminded me of him and I gave him a phone call to tell him I was cycling through Schreiber. He said there had been a monument built there to commemorate the Japanese-Canadian men who had worked in four different road camps nearby. I never did see the monument.

I carried on to Terrace Bay to a campground near the town.

Day 40, Monday, June 9
Distance: 115.98 km in foggy weather along Hwy 11/17 to Pukaskwa National Park

Even with the train and truck traffic, the ongoing rain kept lulling me back to sleep, past my usual 7:30 am start time. I decided to get moving and spend some time at the TIC with free Internet access, hoping for the rain to slow down. The Internet was often my main communication during the days with no cycling partners. I enjoyed the chance to catch up on emails, post blogs and read comments from friends and family. The Terrace Bay Plaza coffee shop was a great place to talk with the locals and to warm up with good coffee and French toast. The rain lightened up ever so slightly, which encouraged me to finally get started cycling. The precipitation was lighter, but it became VERY foggy. At times, I could only see one to two telephone poles away and realized this was not safe. All my bike lights were turned on to increase my visibility to drivers. With all the fog, I was barely able to see the road and traffic, let alone any of the lake views. One advantage of the cool misty weather was fewer bugs at the rest stops.

I took rest stops along the roadside barrier, stretching as I munched. At one point along the highway, I came amazingly close to an adult moose drinking from a roadside pond. By the time I stopped to reach for my camera, it had unfortunately noticed me and fled.

My planned destination for the day was Marathon, named after the lumber company of the same name. There was no TIC so I cycled the 6 km off the highway into town only to find that the only campground was being renovated. I considered staying there anyway, but it seemed too isolated and away from town. At the Extra Foods grocery store, I chatted with a guy who had passed me driving along the highway who told me about other options for camping. The best option seemed to be to keep going south to Pukaskwa National Park, a huge park on the east coast of Lake Superior. This was an opportunity to investigate facilities at a national park for a change. The first thing I noticed was that all the signs were posted in the two official languages (French as well as English). More funding must have been available federally as there were excellent facilities including an appealing visitor centre. Regrettably, the centre was closed for the season. Bear-proof caches were included on the site, so I stashed my food there. Fortunately I was able to have a hot shower at the spotless service centre. Fog was still covering the lake which made the whole park look somewhat eerie.

Day 41, Tuesday, June 10
Distance: 100 km to White River, ON

Initially, I had to don all my winter gear, including mitts, to ward off the cold of the early morning. The highway and landscape were in transition, sometimes just straight and level, otherwise curvy and hilly like Canadian Shield country. The forest was mostly boreal but transitioning to birch/hardwood and red pine/spruce/tamarack.

Signs of human civilization were few on this lonely stretch of highway. Finally I stopped for some coffee and a real breakfast at the first restaurant, Gloria's, about 65 km along the highway from the national park. That gave me enough fuel to get to my day's destination of White River. However, both campgrounds listed in the tourist brochure were no longer in business. The Husky truck stop in the town had clean showers

Snow danger sign near White River, ON; Day 41

for $5 and staff there advised me to camp at the local park right outside the TIC. I took the requisite photos of White River's Winnie the Pooh and large Thermostat monuments. White River claims to be Winnie the Pooh's hometown. The bear on which the stories were based originally came from White River and was named Winnie after Winnipeg. The Thermostat marked the time when White River became known as the coldest spot in Canada recording a temperature of -58°C.

Fortunately, I had just finished eating my restaurant dinner before a power outage hit the whole town. This assisted my decision making about where to stay. As the official campsites were closed, I had considered staying in a motel room. The fact that there was no power meant there was no advantage to that option. Instead I decided to camp in the town park just off the highway. As I did not want my tent to be noticed, I waited for the sun to descend. I sat in the local Robin's donut shop, reading and drinking a juice while waiting for dusk. As the forecast was for rain or snow, I set up my tent in the shelter of the town TIC.

Day 42, Wednesday June 11
Distance: 128.72 km along Hwy 17 past Wawa, ON to Lake Superior Provincial Park

My first stealth tent camping experience in a town park was not too distressing. There were some unsettling human noises around 2:00 am when the bar must have let out. I awoke to some muffled conversations, shuffling feet and the sounds of engines starting up. Thankfully, as far as I knew, nobody came to investigate my shelter, although they may have wondered about it. Luckily it didn't get cold enough to snow, though it was definitely chilly. After I packed up, I washed and ate at the truck stop, near the "campsite".

The day was favourable for cycling: agreeable wind, temperature and hills. There seemed to be more downhill than uphill. After about 60 km, it had started warming up and I was switching to a vest when a group of four touring cyclists passed me, cancer fundraisers in yellow and blue jerseys and shorts. I passed their support van and they passed me again. They chatted to me a bit while cycling and handed me a power bar and power gel. As this was fairly isolated country, there were not many travelers, let alone touring cyclists to meet. It was the highlight of my day, to actually have some cyclists to talk to and cycle (somewhat) with!

I reached Wawa and headed straight to the famous goose at the TIC. Wawa is Ojibway for wild goose. Of course, I had someone take a photo of me with the goose monument. The TIC luckily had Internet service, allowing me to communicate with ex-Ontarians who had worked in Wawa and to my Ottawa friend for birthday greetings. With the lengthening days, there were more daylight hours to reach a destination, making it more relaxing. As towns are few and far between along the Superior shoreline, it meant packing food for future meals. I ate a hot sandwich at a restaurant and bought some food at a grocery store and at Timmy's to pack along.

Wawa Goose and me; Day 42

I headed out again to Hwy 17 south. It seemed odd to be heading south, but that meant the route was past the northernmost point of Lake Superior. Soon, I had passed the entrance sign to Lake Superior Provincial Park. The scenery was very majestic with impressive views of the lakes, veteran trees (especially old white pines) and the winding road. While cycling along, I was reminded of many summers spent working in the forests of northeastern Ontario. My memories were mainly of camping, swimming and certainly, black flies. This was rugged and wild country, a bit too isolated for many. It would have been nice to have a cycling companion on this leg of the route. As I did not, I took advantage of the long days and kept cycling longer distances to the next campground. I reached Rabbit Blanket Lake campsite, where I ate, showered and journaled.

Day 43, Thursday, June 12
Distance: 120 km through Lake Superior Provincial Park to Pancake Bay, ON

The weather started off with showers then eventually the sun came out and I was into t-shirt and shorts. I said hello to three sets of cyclists heading north, which was unusual. Just before reaching a rest stop, I saw a small black bear before he sauntered off into the bush. The park visitor centre at Agawa Bay was quite a beautiful rest stop. I found out that Thunder

North of Superior spruce bog; Day 43

Bay to Wawa is 470 km and that was only a quarter of the way around the whole lake (according to the Lake Superior map). Cycling was fine with many hills and the wind unable to stay in one direction. I was finally able to take many photos of impressive views of the blue lake and rocky shore.

I decided to continue to cycle the next 50 km to Pancake Bay. I kept leapfrogging the four "Typically Canadian" cyclists, which was my entertainment for the day. They would pass me and then stop for a break with their support van. Then I would pass them and I would stop for a break...and the cycle kept going. Near Montreal River, there were some massively steep hills, famous from stories I had heard even in BC. It meant eating a protein gel for

veteran white pine tree north of Superior; day 43

energy and shifting into granny gears to ascend. I had hoped for a small restaurant near the campsite but was disappointed. At least, there was a small store and I had enough food to concoct a dinner. There were not nearly as many black flies as the previous night, possibly due to the wind. The surf-like sound of the lapping waves of the lake was soothing to fall asleep to.

Day 44, Friday, June 13
Distance: 95.882 km along Hwy 17 south to Sault Ste. Marie, ON

There was a huge wind and rain storm overnight and the power was out from Wawa to somewhere beyond Batchawana Bay. One could imagine the storms being disastrous for ships sailing on Lake Superior. Somewhere near Pancake Bay was where the Edmund Fitzgerald ship sank in 1975, which Canadian folksinging legend Gordon Lightfoot wrote a song about. After my breakfast and coffee at Goulais River, I again met the four "Typically Canadian" cyclists. They

Heading towards the Soo with Lake Superior in the background

had passed by and I approached them while they were snacking from their support van at the side of the road. Kyle, Andrew, Steve and Alex were such inspiring young men. They had either just graduated or were still at university and were cycling across Canada, raising funds for cancer research. They gave me their business card and welcomed me to follow their website and blog. They were on somewhat the same route but had a very distinct schedule as they had to meet townspeople and had events to attend. They invited me to join them at the end-of-the-trip celebrations in St. John's NF on July 26, after we discovered we all intended to finish around the same time there!

I passed the midpoint marker of the Trans-Canada Highway and quickly took a photo before being swarmed by black flies. I reached Sault Ste Marie (the Soo) in mid-afternoon and decided to stay at the Glenview campground, with full amenities. I quickly set up camp amidst clouds of annoying mosquitoes then headed into the town. The TIC was huge due to the international bridge which was the border crossing between Canada and the US. The staff gave me directions to the Riverside Bike Trail, which I cycled along to tour the town and to Velorution Bike Shop. This shop stocked many items for touring cyclists like the Schwalbe brand tire that I was looking for. I bought the tire for the Ottawa shop to install when I arrived there. Behind the shop was an unknown (to me) tiny campground, especially convenient for touring cyclists. In front of the shop was a sculpture of a giant bicycle which totally dwarfed my touring bike.

After eating home-made pasta at a very crowded Giovanni's restaurant, I cycled back to the campground to clean up. I especially enjoyed using the spacious mosquito-free game room with lots of table space and other campers to chat with.

Day 45, Saturday, June 14
Distance: 20 km; rented a vehicle to travel to North Bay, ON

Each time I talked to my friend in Ottawa, John kept pressuring me to reach Ottawa days earlier than my planned schedule, to arrive in time for events he wanted me to attend. I decided to rent a vehicle to travel from Sault Ste. Marie to North Bay. Various references had stated that this stretch of the Trans-Canada Highway had unsafe road conditions (poor, eroded shoulders) and heavy traffic near Sudbury. The classmates I had reached in Thessalon and near Sudbury were currently either out of town or incommunicado. The bicycle fit quite handily into the trunk of the Grand Prix full size vehicle with the seats down. It felt quite odd to drive away from the Soo along Hwy 17 East. The hills were rolling and the forestscape was changing from Canadian Shield to Great Lakes forest with much more hardwood in the mix.

After a few hours of driving, I stopped at the Sturgeon Falls TIC for area maps, information and use of their Internet. By the time I reached the National car rental office in North Bay, it was about 3:30 pm, not bad for 442 km. Driving the 700 km from the Soo to North Bay shaved about three cycling days off the schedule. The fellow at the car rental office was able to drive me to the campsite so he could have the car back. He seemed to be in no hurry and enjoyed touring me around the city somewhat en route to the campground. On the way, I noticed a motel with a campground behind it called the Franklin. This campground seemed a much cleaner and safer setup close to the lakeside in the motel district of North Bay. This attractive city was right beside huge Lake Nipissing yet unbelievably, no mosquitoes were bothering me.

After setting up camp at the Franklin, there was time to actually tour around town. I cycled along an excellent bike trail to the downtown waterfront park and garden. North Bay had spent time cleaning up its waterfront, which resulted in beautiful beaches and gardens. It really had improved from the small town I remembered from thirty years previously when visiting classmates. I ate a fancy canneloni farci at the recommended Little Owl Bistro where I chatted with some locals and the staff. The manager generously celebrated my tour by providing a harvest apple cheesecake on the house!

Day 46, Sunday, June 15
Distance: 69.75 km along Hwy 17 to Mattawa, ON

This was another nice cycling day—temperature, winds and sun were all favourable—just around 20°C. I got up early, walked to Timmy's for coffee and breakfast, to the A & P for snacks, then packed up and was on the road by 8:00 am. It's best to leave before the wind changes or the temperature soars.

Rest stops were abundant en route from North Bay to Mattawa. The North Bay TIC on the road leading out of town shared space with a museum of the famous Dionne quintuplets. The museum was housed in the original family homestead but was closed at that time. The museum/TIC was at the junction of Hwy 11 which heads south to southern Ontario/Toronto and north to northeastern Ontario and Hwy 17 which continues east towards Ottawa. My route headed east along Hwy 17 to the appealing Ottawa valley.

After about 40 km, I stopped at the Samuel de Champlain Provincial Park to see their display on Voyageurs. Champlain was a premier explorer of Canada, maybe best known as the Father of New France. Imagining those short, tough fellows travelling and exploring in their birch bark canoes was quite inspirational. One amazing 39-foot replica canoe was on display showing the skill needed to create that means of travel.

From the park to Mattawa was only another 15 km and I stopped at the TIC to determine my camping options. The local Sid Turcotte Park was within walking distance of the river trails and town. I walked around town, viewing the many wooden historic figures. The Golden Age Club was hosting a fundraising "fish fry," frying up fish and chips for the seniors. While eating my fish, I chatted with Armand, a friendly local Robitaille. The Robitaille family had proudly lived in the Ottawa valley for many generations and included a famous NHL player. Before heading back to the campground, I still had time to watch *Narnia* at the movie theatre.

Day 47, Monday June 16
Distance: 106.29 km along Hwy 17 to Deep River, ON in the Ottawa Valley

I packed up and left the campground somewhat late, stopped at Country Style for a coffee and coincidentally met up with Armand again. He bought my breakfast bagel, we chatted a bit and I finally got on the road again around 9:15 am. The terrain was mainly rolling hills with some views of the Ottawa River. Right across the river within view was Québec, a new province to explore!

I passed Driftwood Provincial Park and decided to keep cycling as there were still many hours of daylight left. I stopped at a variety store to get a frozen fruit bar to cool down from the heat. I had a friend Olissia who I had worked with in 1980 in Vancouver and remembered that she was from nearby Deep River. I looked in the phone book at the variety store and, sure enough, her surname Stechishen was there. For the next 25 or 30 km of cycling, I was remembering days working and travelling with Olissia in the early 80s. I called the phone number at the next rest stop, the Rolphton Esso, and reached Olissia's dad, Ed, on the phone. After a short conversation, Ed kindly invited me to stay at their home in Deep River instead of camping. I agreed and got directions to their home. I stowed my bike in their garage, admired their well-manicured garden, met Olga the mom and was invited inside their charming home. Ed was in the midst of making a kitchen full of perogies for a fundraiser. They reached Olissia by phone and I made plans to meet her in Ottawa. The delicious, homemade, hot meal they served was such a treat for me.

Day 48, Tuesday, June 17
Distance: 81.787 km to Cobden, ON

After enjoying a very pleasant bacon and egg breakfast with Ed, Olga and Sam (Olissia's brother) at their home, I took a goodbye photo of my hosts in their thriving garden and said a huge thank you for their kind hospitality. I cycled through some road construction towards Petawawa under cloudy skies that threatened rain. As I passed the Petawawa Forest Centre, it started to drizzle and the Visitor Centre appeared to be closed. Petawawa was the site of the University of Toronto forestry spring camp in my first year of university, but it was not worth cycling down the dirt road to reminisce since the facilities were not open. The road from Deep River to Chalk River was under construction and the rest of the way had very narrow shoulders so I cycled the 7 km off Hwy 17 to get to the main road to Pembroke. After my lunch stop at Timmy's, I cycled through town to see the historic buildings and murals. Storm clouds were building up so I cycled quickly to the TIC to beat the rain. I waited out the storm in a quiet, dry centre, updating the blog, checking the Internet for emails and information and talking to the friendly staff. When there was a break in the weather, I cycled back to the highway, deciding to camp at Cobden. It is a small town right along the highway, in a pleasant rural area of the valley. The Cobden municipal campground was in a park handily right beside the road. I had enough time to wander through the local shops before closing time and ate at one of the restaurants.

Day 49, Wednesday, June 18
Distance: 65 km to Arnprior, ON then to John and
Francine's house in Ottawa, ON

As the campsite was beside the highway, I was awake early, so packed up and was on the road by 7:00 am. I reached a Timmy's at Renfrew by about 9:00 am and gave John, my friend in Ottawa, a call to check in. We agreed to meet at Timmy's at Arnprior about 2:00 pm, which gave me plenty of time. In Renfrew, I cycled to the museum which was, unfortunately, not open. Hidden right beside the museum was a suspension swinging bridge over the Bonnechere River. This unknown site was a scenic find, so I stopped and took a few photos. A fellow at the town hotel suggested going to Arnprior via the (Ottawa) River Road since it was much more scenic and off the main Hwy 17.

Along River Road were some very picturesque views of the Ottawa River. Some development was present, but most of the countryside was rural and undeveloped. I took many photos of historic log barns and homes, many of which were being restored but some that have been the same way for generations. The rain came and went but did not pour while I was cycling. I made it to Arnprior with lots of time so visited the museum in a magnificent historic building. The museum was filled with personal artifacts from logging camps, weaving and natural history.

I headed out towards the Timmy's meeting place and decided this was the

Gillie's Grove maple forest, near Arnprior, Ottawa Valley; Day 49

time to taste some local poutine, often sold from chip stands set up in parking lots. This Québecois epicurean delight, of fries loaded with gravy and fresh cheese curds, sort of sits in your stomach and is not healthy, but it does taste wonderful. Happily, I met John at the scheduled time and place. John is one of my oldest buddies from my university class and every reunion is a joy. He took me on a tour of Gillie's Grove, a local 23 ha forest of old growth white pine, sugar maple, yellow birch, beech and basswood situated right along the Ottawa River. It was a wonderful example of a Great Lakes forest, fitting for two foresters to hike through!

My bike was transported in John's vehicle and taken to the bike shop for a tune-up. In the meantime, I had the luxury of resting and settling into life at John and his wife Francine's residence in Ottawa. We had several years' worth of stories to catch up on.

Day 50, Thursday, June 19
Rest day in Ottawa, ON

It was a thrill to be in the household to help the Beaudin and Hall families celebrate the graduation of their daughter, Gabrielle, from high school. There were a lot of invitees as well as much food and drink. There were even some friends and family whom I knew and was able to chat with, including Mrs. Hall and Olissia, who came to visit. I felt very lucky to have been invited to join in the celebration with John and Francine and their family. John gave a very nice speech congratulating Gabrielle on a job well done.

Day 51-53, Friday, June 20-Sunday, June 22
Recreation Days at a cabin in the Gatineau Hills

John drove a friend and me past downtown Ottawa, across the bridge, northwest to the Gatineau Hills and crossed the Gatineau River on our way to a cabin on a beautiful remote lake. This classic Canadian Shield country was filled with mainly hardwoods, some huge white pine trees and plentiful, clean, clear blue lakes. We

Rest days spent at a lake in the Gatineau Hills, QC; Day 52

stopped at a dam (crossing) to view an old, out-of-commission log chute which had been used to move logs from one lake to another. We arrived at the lake in the early evening. Our task upon arrival was to unload gear from the vehicle, load the small boat to transport gear to the end of the lake where the cabin was and carry the gear to the cabin. The gear included beds (in parts), wood, equipment for working, food, sleeping bags and personal packs. One cabin was just reaching its occupancy stage and this was a work weekend to put the final touches on it. Meals were prepared for the workers and it was all pretty well organized. As the work was quite dusty and dirty, the easiest way to clean off was with a swim in the clear, calm, beautiful blue lake to get refreshed again.

Francine, Gabrielle and Daniel (John's wife and children) drove up to the lake after Francine finished work. Everyone was put to work, though some people were more skilled or interested than others. After the Saturday work was completed, a celebration of the opening of the new structure took place complete with a ribbon-cutting ceremony, bubbly and appetizers. There was also a special banquet to give thanks to all the people who organized and planned for this new cabin. I felt very fortunate to have been invited to come along on that auspicious weekend. Again, there were several speeches and congratulations to the cabin-building committee members.

Day 54, Monday, June 23
Distance: 30 km to MEC and return to the house

After its tune-up, I picked up my bicycle from the bike shop and took it for a test drive out to the Mountain Equipment Co-op (MEC) store and back. The gears, brakes and mechanical adjustments worked just fine. After returning home, Daniel and I found all the ingredients to make sushi and we made up a big batch for everyone for my last evening at their home.

Day 55, Tuesday, June 24
Distance: 19.45 km touring Ottawa, ON tourist sites

I packed up and gave final hugs, farewells and a giant thank-you to John, Francine, Gabrielle and Daniel, my hosts since the previous Wednesday. I certainly counted my blessings to have such warm-hearted, generous friends. My body completely appreciated these six days of rest, good food and relaxation.

I cycled towards town and toured the Museum of Nature near downtown Ottawa. The most interesting part of Ottawa is that the majority of the people on the street are noticeably bilingual. French is such a beautiful language to hear and for me to try to understand.

I met up easily with Nancy and Sheila, my touring partners (from BC) who had arrived in Ottawa the previous night. We met at the Inn at Somerset, the B&B in a restored brick heritage building, our accommodation in Ottawa. Nancy and I had a great time reuniting and it was a pleasure to meet her sister-in-law, Sheila. We dropped gear off then cycled up the street to Parliament Hill. Luckily for us, the weather was excellent for travelling and taking photos. All three of us enjoyed the experience of touring in a new place. We cycled past the war memorial then to the *Marché By* (Byward Market) for lunch. We downed a salad and a large beer, along with plenty of water. We decided to cycle to Rideau Hall to check out the residences of the Prime Minister and Governor General. Rideau Hall and the gardens were open so we cycled along the trails there. While we were there, a limo drove up to the hall delivering a group of women about our age. They appeared to be touring from the southern USA dressed in fancy cocktail dresses and stiletto heels. We took each others' photos in front of Rideau Hall—quite a contrast in appearance. From there we cycled along the Rideau River and the Rideau Canal routes; both were very well used and maintained bicycle paths. We felt fortunate to be able to cycle together along this easy route on such a fair-weather day. Finally, we cycled back to the B&B and got cleaned up, ready to eat out. We ate at an excellent Indian restaurant and sampled their Naan bread which a brochure claimed was the best in Ottawa.

> Lesson learned: it is not always a good idea (for me) to cycle after drinking a large beer.

Ontario Cycling

This province is so large it needs to be divided into sections as each section is different from the other. The northwest Canadian Shield country may be more mentally than physically challenging. The isolation between towns means the cyclist needs to buy (food) supplies when available and hope any technical difficulties encountered en route can be overcome by oneself. The small towns usually offer helpful, friendly folks used to being self-sufficient.

The towns and roads were not bike-unfriendly and Ottawa was very bike friendly. There are many routes across the province and a provincial guidebook or website to summarize cycle touring in the province is definitely lacking. I was anticipating the route north of Superior to be much busier than it was as it is the TC Hwy, along which most of the transport and tourist traffic travels.

My route did not include cycling in the south, unless the beautiful Ottawa valley is considered south. All across the province is a wide range of landscapes, including a great number of clear fresh-water lakes, as well as interesting and diverse ecosystems and vegetation to observe. As I had lived and worked in northern Ontario, I was prepared for the onslaught of mosquitoes and black flies in June, which were still as annoying as thirty years previously.

Ontario Statistics

Distance: 1,480.35 km
Days: 23 including 6 rest days in Ottawa, Gatineau
Tent camping nights: 6 paying, 6 nonpaying
Home accommodation: 9 nights
B&B: 1 night

Ontario

Day	Km	Destination	Route	Notes
35	138	Aaron Prov Park	Hwy 17	boreal forest
36	110.24	Sandbar Lake Prov Park	Hwy 17	boreal forest, moose sighting
37	37.2	Thunder Bay	Hwy 17, road closures	flooding, a helpful drive
38	124	Red Rock	Hwy 11/17	boreal forest
39	118.05	Terrace Bay	Hwy 11/17	north of Lake Superior
40	115.98	Pukaskwa National Park	Hwy 11/17	north of Lake Superior
41	100	White River	Hwy 11/17	north of Lake Superior
42	128.72	Lake Superior Prov Park	Hwy 11/17	north of Lake Superior
43	120	Pancake Bay	Hwy 11/17	north of Lake Superior
44	95.88	Sault Ste Marie	Hwy 11/17	north of Lake Superior
45	20	North Bay	Hwy 11/17	rental vehicle drive
46	69.75	Mattawa	Hwy 17	valley
47	106.29	Deep River	Hwy 17	valley
48	81.787	Cobden	Hwy 17	valley
49	65	Arnprior	Hwy 17	a drive to friends
50	0	Ottawa		rest day
51-53	0	Gatineau Hills		rest days
54	30	Ottawa	testing bike tuneup job	rest day
55	19.45	Ottawa	touring Ottawa city	touring
	1480.35	Ontario total kms		

Ontario

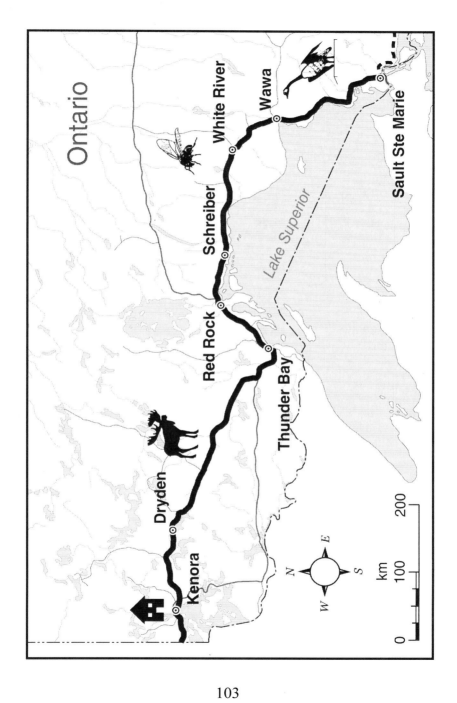

103

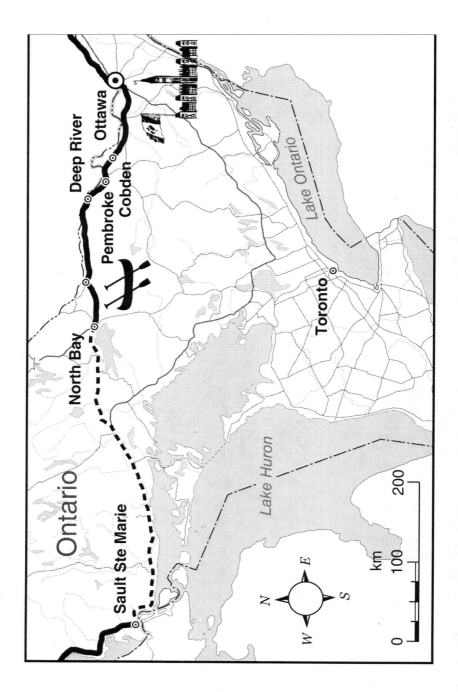

Chapter 5
La Belle Province, Québec

Day 56, Wednesday, June 25
Distance: 55.5 km to Thurso, QC

The tasty breakfast at the B&B was such luxury! After packing up, Nancy, Sheila and I retrieved the bikes and determined our route. We crossed the Ottawa River on the Alexandra Bridge and took photos of each other with Parliament Hill in the background. Excellent views of Ottawa were visible from that vantage point. Separate pathways for pedestrians and cyclists made that bridge safe to traverse.

Departing over the Ottawa River with the city of Ottawa in the background; Day 56

Ottawa is a very cycling-friendly and tourist-friendly city.

On the north side of the bridge, as we crossed into the province of Québec, official "Welcome to Quebec" signs were nowhere to be seen. We took photos of each other beside a memorial statue of Maurice "Rocket" Richard, a legendary Québecois hockey player icon. Following that, we were into Jacques Cartier Park and we found a Route Verte sign. We ended up following the Route Verte (green route), the official bicycle route throughout the province. It is the most extensive cycling network of "marked paths, paved shoulders and designated roadways" in all of North America and has won numerous awards, including first in the National Geographic Society Best Bicycle route in the world.

We followed the Gatineau Park pathway all along the river, except for one navigational error at an intersection. After crossing the bridge into Québec, we found most people spoke French with a bit of English. Luckily, Sheila was quite fluent in French and was able to ask questions and translate for us. At first we were still on a pathway in a park, then it became a back road off the main route, and in the end we were on the main highway headed east towards Montreal. Groundhogs were seen along the road and in the park. Many St. Lawrence Lowland hardwood forest species abounded

The Québec Route Verte with Nancy and Sheila; Day 56

including red oaks, white pines, basswoods and others. There were also very interesting wildflowers along the roadsides. These were tree species that I remembered studying at university but rarely ever saw in real life. Besides the language difference, there already seemed to be a difference in culture in this province. There were many more cigarette smokers and there seemed to be more young mothers (pushing strollers).

We cycled along the highway, paralleling the Ottawa River, along La Route Verte 1 to Thurso, a town right on the route. We stopped at an intersection in the small town to discuss camping at the national Parc de Plaisance, as the map book was not clear if there was camping there. A local fellow, named Billy, approached and asked in English if we needed directions. He said there was no camping in the park, but we were welcome to stay in his yard, as he owned a nearby seniors' home and had plenty of space there. We cycled to the end of the road at the river's edge and checked out his property. The acreage had large well-maintained lawns, clean washrooms and was close to town so we made the decision to camp there. We returned to a diner in town to eat and make phone calls and shopped at the grocery store. We brought beer back to the campsite for our host and chatted with Billy's partner, Gwen. She was full of stories, reminiscing about life in a small Québec town.

Day 57, Thursday, June 26
Distance: 71.7 km along Hwy 148 past Grenville, QC

We broke camp and said thank you and goodbye to Billy and Gwen before heading to the Parc Nationale de Plaisance. Parc Nationale in Québec means a provincial park, not a national park. A Parcs Québec worker in a pick-up truck drove up to warn us that we were heading towards a dead end and the ferry ahead departed only at 12:45 pm! As we were not about to wait several hours for a small ferry, we decided to backtrack a few kilometres and head north to Hwy 148 E. We ate a "real" breakfast at Plaisance, continued on to Papineauville where we bought fruit, and then to Montebello where we stopped to tour the wonderful log lodge now owned by the Fairmont group. It seemed to be used for conference facilities with a fitness centre, spa, restaurant and excellent group facilities. Sheila had memories of visiting there many years previously. An amazingly huge six-sided stone fireplace had been built in the centre to heat the structure.

We continued east along the Route Verte 1/Hwy 148 and stopped at an ice cream *bar laitier* for what became our daily snack of ice cream and GORP. Under threatening skies, we cycled on to Grenville, where there was a very friendly and helpful TIC. Luckily, we reached the LeVieux Bistro in town before a thunderstorm hit and the skies opened up. We ate

Puddles during a Québec downpour; Day 57

quite cozily indoors while watching some huge lightning strikes, including an enormous one that shook the restaurant. The cars passing by in front of the window were soon swimming in puddles above the tops of their tire wheel wells. Some of these Québec storms were very sudden and violent but passed by very quickly. We waited for the storm to pass, then went to the local market to buy fruit. We heard that lightning had struck a greenhouse right behind that market, knocking the power out in the neighbourhood. That was a close call! We cycled 15 km towards Carillon to the municipal campground. It had all the amenities, including laundry and showers, and we even went for a quick swim at the small beach there.

Day 58, Friday, June 27
Distance: 67.68 km to Laval, QC

Before going to sleep, there were shuffling sounds as Nancy and Sheila were being visited by raccoons trying to munch on trail mix that had accidentally fallen from its packaging! In the morning, we broke camp and had snacks (before the raccoons returned) and cycled towards Carillon. We visited the Carillon Canal National Historic Site, showing the importance of the canals built in 1812 and also site of the largest hydro-electric dam in Québec. There was no restaurant in sight, so caffeine-deprived Nancy kept us cycling to St. André d'Argenteuil for a diner breakfast and coffee.

After breakfast, we found our way back to Hwy 344, right along the Ottawa River. We passed Oka and the Parc Nationale d'Oka right along the highway. This was a very busy section of the highway where there were many First Nations outlets selling discount cigarettes. Along that section, my bicycle started making unusual grinding sounds. The sounds were really odd and I was examining my gears on the roadside when a local cyclist stopped by to lend a hand. He called himself a "cycling ambassador," did not know what the strange noise was either but gave us directions and led us partway to the closest bicycle shop just beyond the *parc*. He gave us a tour en route, showing us where the Oka security incident happened in July 1990. There had been a clash between 200 Mohawk Nation people and a developer. The Mohawk people claimed the golf course the developer was building was expanding onto native burial grounds. The Québec police and the Canadian army finally were involved in an incident that drew worldwide attention to the rights of First

Nations people. We cycled on some wonderful bike trails through the *parc* and chatted with some cyclists who had taken the train from Montreal and were cycling in the opposite direction to us. I was very fortunate being able to cycle right to the Grange Bicycle Shop in St-Marthe-sur-le-Lac. A different "ambassador" cyclist led us directly there, right along the bike route. The shop had to replace the bearings and luckily that humble shop in that small town had the parts in stock. While waiting for the service, we tested the local ice cream at an excellent *bar laitier* and cooled off at the first Tim Horton's we'd seen in Québec. Fortunately, the repair job was finished in a couple of hours and we were able to continue on our way.

We returned to the Route Verte heading east through Deux Montagnes and over a bridge towards Laval. Nancy had spent many hours researching accommodations on the

Québec sign to share the road with cars and bicycles; Day 58

Internet while at home. We found our way to the Auberge-les-Menus-Plaisirs along Blvd Ste Rose, a bicycle-friendly inn in Laval listed in the Route Verte book. As the name suggests, this auberge was also a lovely restaurant, and the proprietor's wife, Martine, took great pleasure in parading three sweaty cyclists past the elegant diners on the way to our room. Nancy rested her Achilles and used the tub, while Sheila and I walked through the interesting neighbourhood and bought some fresh sushi and beer for take-out. We enjoyed using the luxurious facilities in the room while eating our late dinner.

Day 59, Saturday June 28
Distance: 57 km through Montreal, QC to Repentigny, QC

The continental breakfast at the *auberge* was delicious and we spent time chatting with Martine, as she kept us supplied with croissants and coffee. She spoke English quite well with her charming Francophone accent and was very down-to-earth relating her stories of planting trees in northern British Columbia. We retrieved our bikes from the garage and cycled past the train station via the Route Verte, alongside the train tracks. The route really was very green, especially considering we were cycling through a major urban centre. We were able to make our way along the Route Verte right to the Maison des Cyclistes, a café/cycling resource centre where we had arranged to meet my brother-in-law Pat, (whom I had met already in Winnipeg). He was full of advice about touring in Québec but not necessarily via bicycle. He gave us a culinary gift of a baguette, some *Québecois* cheese and a bottle of wine—how French! Sheila cycled to a nearby bike shop to see if they could reset her handlebar angle to relieve her sore wrists.

We were on bicycles again by around 4:30 pm, along Rene Levesque then Notre Dame Blvd. All the towns along the Saint Lawrence River seem to have a Notre Dame Blvd and a Rue de Quai. We passed alongside the real Port of Montreal, lost the route for a bit, eventually found it again and had to cross another bridge to depart the city and end up on the north side of the river again. The rain started pelting down so we decided to find accommodation in Charlemagne. We discovered that Charlemagne is the birthplace of Celine Dion and we ended up staying at the Hotel Charlemagne on Celine Dion Road. Supper was at the St. Hubert restaurant where we were entertained by a singer singing French songs known by many of the locals. We then returned to our quiet room (out of the rain) and finished off the cheese, baguette and wine from Pat, inspired to buy local food in Québec.

Day 60, Sunday, June 29
Distance: 84.184 km along Route Verte 5 to St Barthélemy, QC

Life on the road with two cycling mates turned out to be remarkably favourable. We discovered some "rules" about each other. We needed to have caffeine as early as possible but at least by 11 am. The ice cream *bar laitier* had become a daily ritual to entice us to reach our destination, as the rule was no ice cream until at least the 60 km mark. We had been dallying a bit too long chatting over breakfast so we were trying to break the habit and get an earlier start. We had a quick continental breakfast at the hotel then tried to get started around 9:15 am. We knew our course along the Route Verte at the beginning, but somehow, even though we kept following the signs, we ended up going in circles. Nancy noticed some landmarks that she was sure we had passed before, and she

Cycling along a Québec secondary route

was right! A fellow cyclist advised us to stay alongside the St. Lawrence River all the way to Québec City, so we followed that advice. We were relieved to reach the far side of the big city and return to the small picturesque towns and rural areas.

From Charlemagne, we cycled to Lavaltrie and stopped at a *boulangerie* to buy some fresh baguettes and fruit to have with the Buchon cheese we had left from what Pat had given us. We stopped near Berthierville for a small picnic. We asked at the TIC to determine our destination campground, about 5 km north of St. Barthélemy. We were hoping to find an ice cream *bar laitier* to relieve the heat but no luck, so we continued on to the campground. The Vieux Moulin was a very busy family campground with an outdoor pool full of patrons. After setting up the tents and throwing in a load of laundry, we jumped into the pool for a refreshing dip. An earnest young girl was trying to communicate to us, using hand signals and French (Sheila had opted not to swim so Nancy and I didn't have our translator). In the end, we figured out that we were supposed to wear these bathing caps that looked like shower caps. We collected and donned the caps, gave the little girl a thumbs-up sign and were rewarded with a big smile. Excellent hot showers followed the swim. The fast food restaurant right beside the pool was handy so we sat and ate while watching another huge lightning storm—better watching it than cycling in it. We went to bed early, sleeping amidst an overnight thunderstorm.

Day 61, Monday, June 30
Distance: 94.219 km along Route Verte 5 to Batiscan

The café was open when we were departing so we decided to stay and enjoy our eggs, toast and coffee and let our bodies warm up. We took the Route Verte to Maskinonge then to Louiseville, went to the IGA and bought a small baguette, cheese, strawberries and yogurt. We lunched near the edge of Lac St. Pierre, such a picturesque spot. We cycled past rural farms that were all 62 feet wide and very long, all the way to the St. Lawrence River, created when the area was first settled 400 years ago. These farms, called *seigneuries*, were originally land grants from France to help establish a French presence in Canada. The farmhouses and outbuildings were built along Québec's agricultural roads forming small communities. This rural fairly level land full of local farm produce made for pleasurable cycling.

We passed through Trois Rivieres where we stopped only at the TIC to get maps and information, although there was much more to explore. There

really were not three rivers but the town got its name from the explorers who thought there were. We cycled on to Champlain

Quebec strawberry stand sign; Day 61

and stopped for delicious strawberry sundaes with fresh strawberries from the neighbouring field. Strawberry season certainly is an excellent time to cycle in Québec!

We continued on the Route Verte 5, which followed the north edge of the St. Lawrence River, to Batiscan, a very beautiful village, with quaint stone houses and painted wooden structures. They had a very informative TIC where they informed us about camping at the nearby marina—what a great idea! However, cycling on the bridge across the Batiscan River to reach the campground was a scary experience. The bridge had an open metal decking and it felt like the bike tires were getting caught in the ruts. Once across, we quite enjoyed the campground with its handy showers, restaurant and neighbouring boats.

Day 62, Tuesday, July 1, Canada Day
Distance: 97 km to Québec City, QC

We cycled 7 km to Ste Anne-de-la-Pérade for a hearty local diner breakfast, then on through picturesque rural Québec—many strawberry stands, fruit and veggie markets, lots of very old structures and very green and lush farms after all the recent rains. On our way into the small town of Grondines, a gardening woman waved us down exclaiming some French greetings. She had stopped us to give us some lovely peonies from her garden, maybe on behalf of Canada Day. She chatted away to us in French and even Nancy understood some of the conversation, successfully miming a joke and feeling quite proud of herself.

The rest of Canada had a Canada Day holiday, but in Québec, there wasn't the same holiday atmosphere. A bakery was open along the main street, where we stopped to buy cookies. The Metro grocery store was open, and we bought the customary yogurt, cheese and baguette for lunch. Our picnic stop was in the shade of some trees, along with a lovely breeze from the river. All along the route were many relatively old barns and historic buildings to observe while cycling along. Signs of recreational activity were evident including parasailing, boating and ice fishing. There were colourful shacks for ice-fishing rentals. The Route Verte had some strange twists and turns, which were fine for local cycling but not always convenient when trying to reach a destination on tour. One example was a huge steep descent to a valley followed by a similarly steep climb back to the same route! We were not impressed!

That day's *bar laitier* break was near Saint-Augustin-de-Desmaure alongside the St. Lawrence where the area displayed some wonderful views of the river. One more great climb out of Cap Rouge, then a final 20 km to our destination B&B in Québec City. We arrived at our awesome castle-like

accommodation, Chateau des Tourelles, around 6:00 pm. The chateau was a quaint, recently renovated and well-furnished B&B well located within walking distance of the old town of Québec. We ate at a nearby restaurant along Rue St. Jean,

Touring Quebec City via bicycle with Nancy and Sheila; Day 63

bought some wine at a neighbouring variety store and drank it on the roof *terrasse*, catching glimpses of the magnificent light show (more on that later). This province totally feels like a different country, with different food, drink, language and culture. Where else in Canada is it possible to buy beer and wine at a variety store?

Day 63, Wednesday, July 2
Distance: 6 km, touring day in the old city of Québec

Touring around the old city on bicycle is a more sensible mode of travel than walking around town. We were able to cycle along many more of the 400-year-old narrow streets stopping at the touristy shops for souvenirs. We visited the historic Chateau Frontenac and toured the facilities then headed outside the walled city to a new walkway along the

Road inside the walled city of Québec;
Day 63

river, called the Promenade de Samuel Champlain, which included a new bicycle path. We took advantage of the many photo opportunities and cycled along the path to the market for our lunch of fresh local bread, cheese, fruit and some pastries. After shopping at the 400 Shop for souvenirs of the 400th birthday of the city, we cycled back to the Tourelles for a rest. In the early evening, we went to Victor's for the best burgers in Québec along with local Barbarel beer. After dinner, we walked to the city wall to get a spot to watch *The Image Mill*. This was the world's largest outdoor light show, projected from more than 30 projectors onto a giant "screen" of concrete grain silos in the harbour. This forty-minute show was amazing, depicting the history of the city for the past 400 years, created especially for the 400th anniversary. The audio was broadcast on a local FM radio station, audible on an MP3 player.

Day 64, Thursday, July 3, 400th anniversary celebrations of Québec City, QC
Distance: 12 km from city to suburbs

The day dawned grey and it started raining by breakfast. We were lucky that our schedule allowed Nancy, Sheila and me to stay this extra day to celebrate the actual 400th anniversary day. Unfortunately, we were no longer able to stay at the Tourelles and had to change accommodations to a motel near the Pont de Québec. For the morning, we packed up all our gear and moved it into the garage with our bicycles. As we wandered down Rue St. Jean looking for open shops and refuge from the rain, we found an excellent bike shop with a private bicycle museum. The owner had collected bicycle paraphernalia from his travels around the world and put it on display. There were photos of him performing stunts on his large front-wheeled bike. If he had been born in a different era, he would be a Cirque du Soleil performer by the sounds of it. On that particular day, he was performing in some city birthday celebrations. We were still there at 11 am when church and other bells rang out in Québec City and across the country in honour of the 400th birthday celebrations.

I was keeping in touch via Blackberry with Brian Q, a friend from Victoria, who said the rain would let up by 1:00 pm, which it did, amazingly. We had to move our gear from the garage to the motel, quite a bit farther west of town. Unfortunately, our new accommodation was quite a seedy motel as there was not a lot of choice on this busy occasion. We ended up taking the shuttle bus back to town, as that appeared to be the most efficient mode of transport for this celebration night. As the rain caused a venue change for some of the concerts we had planned on attending, we toured the Bluenose sailboat that was docked in the harbour.

After some messaging, we managed to meet up with Brian Q. and some friends at the harbourfront. What a thrill to have an unplanned rendezvous in Québec City with a fellow forester from Victoria. We chatted with them for a bit, Sheila practising her French with Eric and Gilbert. As with most fireworks displays, eventually a huge crowd of spectators arrived. During the wait, a local woman was lamenting that she had never left Québec because she felt her spoken English was not adequate. I had a tough time understanding her heavily-accented French, but we were able to communicate. Finally, we witnessed an unbelievable display of fireworks that seemed to last a very long time. However, the memory of a very frustrating, unorganized return to the motel via shuttle outweighed the memory of the fireworks display. We did not get back to the motel and into bed until about 3:00 am. Sheila and Nancy had to leave around 7:30 am to catch flights to their next destination. We said very tired and sad goodbyes as they dismally loaded their bikes and themselves into a very small cab.

Day 65, Friday, July 4
Distance: 95.3 km along Route Verte 1 to L'Islet-sur-Mer, QC

This was another excellent cycling day, favourable temperature, about 24°C, and some tailwind. I cycled the Route Verte along Blvd Champlain east to the ferry that crosses the St. Lawrence River to Levis. The ferry was easy to board, quick and offered extensive views of Québec City, especially the Chateau, the harbour and the grain silos. On the Levis side, there was a cyclists' cafe right beside the ferry terminal, along with a TIC—very handy. The Route Verte continued for quite a ways along the south side, making it amenable to many cyclists. All along the route were fields of dairy cows, working farms and panoramic views of the St. Lawrence River. It appeared the dairy industry was alive and well here. I was wishing Nancy and Sheila could have stayed on to tour this part of Québec as well.

My next stop was at a Montmagny cycle shop to get my air pressure checked and search for a Louis Garneau product (as Louis Garneau is produced in Québec), finally settling on an LG bathing suit. While in the local TIC waiting out another thunderstorm, I was able to use the Internet and call home. During my stay in Ontario, I discovered that long distance calling cards were the easiest and cheapest way to keep in touch with family at home and elsewhere. I reached L'Islet-sur-Mer, where, luckily, there was a municipal campground on the route. This village had made it onto the list of the Most Beautiful Villages in Québec, an association created to preserve the architectural and historical heritage of villages in Québec. The campground was an excellent site with magnificent views of the sun setting over the St. Lawrence River, a pub with live entertainment just off-site, as well as an outdoor movie playing in the park next door. The film was dubbed in French, which I tried to understand.

Day 66, Saturday, July 5
Distance: 115.47 km to Rivière-du-Loup, QC

Stone house in rural Quebec

L'Islet-sur-Mer is a beautiful, quaint village, full of historic traditional houses that are hundreds of years old. Now that my time was my own, I took photos and tried to fill my memory banks with many typical Québec scenes: the bar laitier, the historic buildings with their unusual rooflines, the traditional wooden swinging chairs, the views of the St. Lawrence River and the vegetable storage bins in the middle of farmers' fields. Rather than the major Hwy 20, I cycled along the secondary Rte 132, which had less traffic but did zigzag quite a bit. There were a few sections that the *La Route Verte* book calls *non-aménagé* (unmanageable), but I managed them. The route followed along the south side of the St. Lawrence River, with many stops indicating historical significance. Many of the towns have been around since the explorers first came to Canada. I picnicked and snacked here and there near Saint-Denis. I

passed through the town of Kamouraska, where they had filmed the movie of the same name. The folks at the TIC in Kamouraska and then at Rivière-du-Loup were helpful for maps and camping information. My main route decision to get to New Brunswick was either via Rivière-du-Loup and south to Edmunston or via Rimouski to try to see Isabel, an underwater hockey teammate when we both played for Team Canada in

Typical Bar Laitier in rural Québec

the World Championships in Sheffield, England. While sitting at the Rivière-du-Loup campground journaling, a fellow cyclist approached and we started chatting. Amazingly, it was Bob from Kamloops whom I had met on Day 2 en route to Cultus Lake. He and wife Joan were cycling across the country (for her retirement celebration) and were headed towards Rimouski then to NB on a similar schedule. That helped firm my decision to first head to Rimouski and then on to New Brunswick.

Day 67, Sunday, July 6
Distance: 112.42 km to Rimouski, QC

The campground had been very busy and noisy but surprisingly became suddenly quiet by 11 pm, which meant a good sleep. I awoke at 7:00 am, had *pain doré* (French toast) and *café* at a local restaurant and was on my way by about 8:30 am, trying to beat the heat of the day. Towns were not as quaint as l'Islet. The landscape was becoming much hillier, rocky and more forested as opposed to agricultural. Along with the scorching heat, the increase in forest cover translated to plentiful bugs again. The river was widening and opening up to a delta as it got closer to the ocean. Many of the local town names began with Saint — not sure of the significance.

At the Trois Pistoles TIC, the staff was very helpful trying to locate Isabel's home phone number, albeit unsuccessful. I finally emailed British Columbia underwater hockey mates, Mel and Jeannie, as a last ditch effort to uncover Isabel's home contact information. At St-Fabien-sur-Mer, I noticed my left shoulder was blistering from the sun and considered stopping. Nearby was a national (provincial) Parc du Bic, with camping. Stopping at a *bar laitier* to cool off with ice cream helped make my decision easier. I decided to make Rimouski my destination and find Isabel to avoid later being disappointed that I did not try my hardest to contact her.

I made a stop at a local *fromagerie* (cheese factory) en route for snacks and finally clocked in at the Rimouski TIC about 5:30 pm. The TIC recommended a nearby CEGEP, which was cheap student accommodation. I showered, then cycled about the picturesque town looking for food, and finally returned to the CEGEP to check my email. It turned out that Mel had responded with Isabel's phone number! I phoned and fortunately Isabel was actually at home available to chat. Isabel had tried to contact me at a different email address, which I had not checked for awhile. She was able to drive to town and we met for tea at a local café, la Brûlerie. We were both thrilled to see each other as this was the only chance to meet. We caught up on the latest underwater hockey news as she had just traveled to the 2008 World Championships in

South Africa. We tried to converse in French, but her English was more fluent than my French so we switched to English. She said that Rimouski had had five metres of snow in the winter of 2008, hard to imagine on that hot July day.

Day 68, Monday, July 7
Distance: 116.36 km to Amqui, QC

I saw Bob and Joan at the Timmy's in Rimouski and for the rest of the day kept leapfrogging them. We seemed to be on the same schedule so it didn't feel like I was cycling alone. I took a detour along the river to view the historic lighthouse and visitor centre at Pointe-au-Père. It was a delight to be right along the river again for my last day of the South of the St. Lawrence River section of the Route Verte (Bas Saint Laurent). I passed through St. Luce, which is the town where Isabel lives. The rural countryside is so attractive alongside the river. I followed the Rte 132, which eventually turned south and east at St-Flavie towards Mont-Joli and away from the river towards New Brunswick. The landscape became more hilly and forested as the route crossed the Gaspé Peninsula along the Matapedia Valley. This valley separates the peninsula from the rest of Québec. I had been anticipating and unsure about major elevation changes while crossing the peninsula, but it was not a concern in the end. The weather and wind were cooperating so I continued on past Sayabec, passed the large lake, Lac Matapedia, and then cycled to Amqui to find a campground. The TIC staff was very friendly and as there were no other tourists, I used the Internet station for awhile, updating the blog and checking emails. I cycled around the quaint town with its historic covered bridge and used the facilities at Camping Amqui: laundry, a refreshing swim in the pool and hot showers.

Day 69, Tuesday, July 8
Distance: 102.85 km to Pointe-à-la-Croix, QC

I saw Bob and Joan early on as I headed for a final *pain doré* breakfast at a canteen. Rain was predicted so I kept cycling. I stopped at the TIC at Causapscal for information and to put in my contact lenses. Hills were increasing with fewer towns and amenities. The route followed the mostly forested Matapedia River valley. I made a stop at St. Florence to view the famous Guinness World Book of Records Largest Fishing Fly. This region is world renowned for fly fishing and someone from the area created the record-breaking fishing fly, a beautiful work of art. I also took a photo of a giant chair at the entrance to the town. Historic covered bridges crossed the Matapedia River at various points, seemingly covered for snow protection. I cycled on to Matapedia, had an ice cream break and chatted with a group of about nine who were cycling from Joliette to the Iles-de-la-Madeleine with a support van. They cycled as a group taking daily turns as driver of the support van, an efficient and budget-friendly approach.

I cycled to Pointe-à-la-Croix, member of the Most Beautiful Bays in the World Club, and the westernmost point of the Baie des Chaleurs, which means Bay of Warmth. The TIC gave me a map of Campbellton and I started planning a route through the next province.

Cycling in Québec

This province surely is "La Belle Province" and is far and away the most bike-friendly province in the country. Like Ontario, it is so large it needs to be divided into sections. The only part I cycled and can comment on is the route along the St. Lawrence River. Cycling in Québec is a treat with many special bike lanes, special traffic lights, parking for bikes, bike-friendly restaurants and accommodations with special storage

124

for bikes. La Route Verte has justifiably won prestigious international awards for its cycling network across the province. The route is well laid out, well marked and well documented both online and in its handy practical guidebook, in both official languages. I was carrying the French version of the guidebook and was able to follow the maps quite easily. The French language, food, drink and culture make this province feel like a different country within Canada. I felt sorry to leave this province to continue my journey.

Québec Statistics

Distance: 1,087.68 km
Days: 14 including 2 rest days in Québec City
Tent camping nights: 7 (all paying)
B&B: 3 nights
Motel or hotel: 2 nights
CEGEP accommodation: 1 night
Oth

Québec

Day	Km	Destination	Route	Notes
56	55.5	Thurso	Route Verte 1, Hwy 148	bicycle trail to hwy
57	71.7	Grenville	Hwy 148	highway
58	67.7	Laval	Hwy 344	bike-friendly
59	57	Repentigny	Notre Dame Blvd, bike routes thru Montreal	busy, bike-friendly
60	84.2	St Barthélemy	Route Verte 5, Hwy 138	bike-friendly
61	94.2	Batiscan	Route Verte 5, Hwy 138	bike-friendly
62	97	Québec City	Route Verte 5, Hwy 138	scenic, rural
63	6	Québec City	Touring Québec City	quaint
64	12	Québec City	Touring Québec City	400th bday Québec
65	95.3	L'Islet sur Mer	Route Verte 1, Hwy 132	charming
66	115	Rivière du Loup	Route Verte 1, Hwy 132	valley
67	112	Rimouski	Route Verte 1, Hwy 132	valley
68	116	Amqui	Route Verte 1, Hwy 132	hilly
69	103	Pointe-à-la-Croix	Route Verte 1, Hwy 132	hilly
	1088	Québec total kms		

Québec

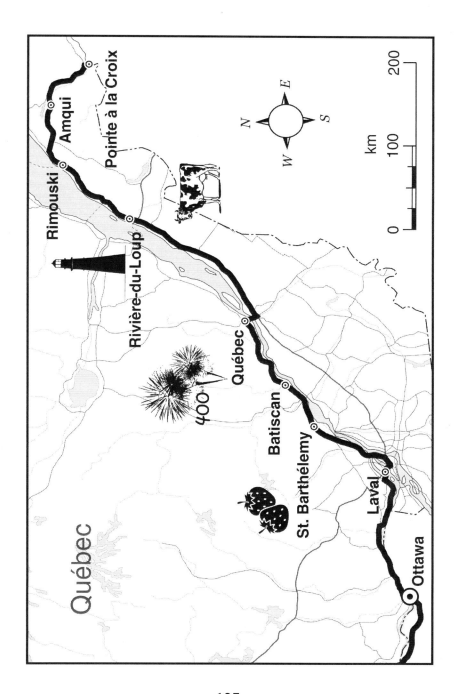

127

Chapter 6
The Maritime Provinces
and the East Coast

Day 70, Wednesday, July 9
Distance: 104.84 km to Nigadoo, NB

I woke up early, dreading crossing the interprovincial bridge over the Restigouche River from Pointe-à-la-Croix, QC to Campbellton, NB. The early morning interprovincial traffic was not heavy, but I concentrated on the road, preventing myself from taking in views of the water below. The mental concentration relieved me of thinking about the length of the bridge and I reached New Brunswick before I knew it. This was Acadian New Brunswick where Acadian French is spoken. New Brunswick already seemed different from Québec: less road maintenance meaning greater potholes, no *laitiers* and a noticeable lack of mileage signs for the next towns, at least on the secondary roads.

The Campbellton TIC was able to provide free Internet and information, but I was surprised at yet another time zone change, my fourth on this tour. New Brunswick and the Maritime Provinces (except Newfoundland) are on Atlantic Time. The difference between British Columbia time and New

Brunswick time is four hours, important information for making phone calls home.

I cycled along the secondary route skirting the north coast and got somewhat turned around in Dalhousie, ending up circling back into town. When I asked a fellow for directions, he recognized me from my loop and tried to give directions, then said, "Throw your bike in my truck," and gave me a ride right out of town, all the way to Charlo. It surprised me that this fellow with a very thick French accent only spoke English. I guess it was the way he had learned to speak with many bilingual friends and neighbours surrounding him. He gave me a lift that was maybe 10 km, bypassing a Micmac reserve, as well as some annoying bridge construction.

After Pointe Verte, there were many homes displaying the Acadian flag. This flag looks somewhat like the French flag with a yellow star set on the blue stripe. At a park at Petit Rocher was a plaque explaining the Acadian history, all new to me. The Acadians have traditional cultural roots that extend to the first French explorers and have kept the Francophone culture alive in north and eastern New Brunswick, as well as other parts of the Maritimes.

Forestry used to be the main industry in the area, but the main Bowater Mill at Dalhousie was shutting down at the time (2008). As viewed from the roads, the forests were becoming depleted of conifers and could no longer support the industry. At Petit Rocher, I quickly grabbed some groceries as a storm was fast approaching. I cycled as fast as I could to the Hache campground at the small town of Nigadoo. My tent was set up in record time. After showering, I took shelter in the camp canteen before a serious thunderstorm arrived and rain came pelting down.

Unfortunately, when I returned to my tent after the rain had stopped, I discovered my small portable shelter resting in a large puddle of rainwater. Water was seeping in from the bottom and the tent and contents were slowly flooding! I had to act fast before all my dry belongings, including a camping mat and down sleeping bag, were all soaked. I moved the dry goods onto a nearby picnic table and had to quickly move the tent to higher territory. I ran to the washroom several times to get piles of paper towels to sop up the inside of the tent. A curious neighbour, who had been in the shower and heard me running in, kindly came by to ask if I needed any towels. She generously lent me an old towel and an old quilt to lay on the bottom of the tent under my camping mat. What an angel! It certainly saved the day and I was so grateful to her. I was able to sleep soundly knowing that both my gear and I were dry.

Day 71, Thursday, July 10
Distance: 85.533 km along Hwy 8 to Miramichi, NB; 95% humidity

I returned the neighbour's quilt and towel to her RV and wished I could thank her again. Cycling to Beresford, I stopped at the first Timmy's for my breakfast bagel and coffee. At the Bathurst TIC, I tried to get information, but in the end I used my own maps to determine directions. The staff was barely able to give me the correct route out of town.

Between Bathurst and Miramichi is mostly scrub forest, although signs indicated past silvicultural treatments. Not many conifers were left, although there was one mill still operating there. The road was paved, but much of it was under construction with huge grade differences between the shoulder and road, not the easiest for cycling. At one point along the highway was a memorial to a local basketball team that had been killed in a driving accident in a recent winter.

The sun was beating down creating very humid conditions, with nary a highway barrier to lean a bicycle against. At the first restaurant, I stopped for water and ice cream. Not much later, a pickup stopped and a local, Tim, offered me a ride to Miramichi, another 26 km away. I accepted and he drove me right to the Timmy's along the highway. It gave me a needed break from the heat. A worker there told me there was a local campground not too far south of town. I happened to meet up and chat with Bob and Joan, who were staying in a motel right around the corner at Miramichi.

Miramichi used to be two cities on either side of the Miramichi River. They were joined when the Centennial Bridge was built to cross the river. The bridge was quite huge and intimidating to cross. Beginning the ascent, I told myself to focus, go slowly and not to look down at the water, as it seemed I could flip right over the side. The TIC was on the south side of town, so I was glad I had continued. I was very close but decided not to follow my original plan to go to Baie Ste Anne to stay with a Victoria friend's mother. This decision was made because it would have added on quite a bit of coastline and distance to get to future destinations. I was able to use the TIC Internet service, updating the blog and enjoying the air-conditioned respite. The staff was very helpful, feeding me some donated sandwiches and calling the All Night All Day Campground for me to get an exact distance to their site. I cycled to the campground and had a very refreshing swim in the pool—so nice to cool off after a day cycling in the heat.

Day 72, Friday, July 11
Distance: 107.58 km along Hwy 11 then 134 to Cocagne, NB

The campground owners were a charming older couple, who also owned a quaint bed and breakfast on site. The woman made me a custom breakfast of boiled eggs, homemade jam, toast and coffee for $5. I cycled away by about 8:45 am and soon met Bob and Joan by the edge of the highway fixing a flat tire. Bob was very proficient at changing the tire and had a very efficient mini-pump. I cycled off while there was a great tailwind and didn't see them again that day. I stopped at Timmy's in Richibucto, but the people gave an unfriendly impression, so I bought some dried snacks and continued cycling to the next town. The long daylight hours and cycling alone allowed me the flexibility to decide where and when to make stops for rest and overnight breaks. The trip was made even more enjoyable by nice wide shoulders, a good tailwind, temperatures that were more moderate and not too many hills.

I cycled on to Bouctouche to another Timmy's. At the entrance to each town in New Brunswick, Tim Horton's is the first recognizable icon the visitor sees. Stopping for a coffee and chatting to the locals was a good introduction to the town and its people. Several restored antique cars were in the Timmy's parking lot on their way to a car show in Moncton. The car show was the 8th annual Atlantic Nationals.

Typical New Brunswick-style lighthouse

Bouctouche is a picturesque coastal town with a very helpful TIC right across the road from a lobster bar. Apparently, people drive from miles around to eat the local "lobster roll". This is fresh lobster spread into a roll, somewhat like a tuna sandwich using lobster instead of tuna—quite a tasty treat! From Bouctouche, I cycled along the old Hwy 134 south to Cocagne to the next campground. At the town, I crossed a four-span historic bridge with a working lighthouse next door. The campground I had planned to stay at was another 10 km away, so I decided to return to the TIC, talk to the fellow and stay at the nearby Acadian campground. My camping neighbours were very kind. After talking to a woman who had a son living on Vancouver Island, she gave me fresh strawberries that she had just picked. I had a 75-cent shower, waited for the sunlight to strike the picturesque 4-span bridge and took some artistic photos.

Day 73, Saturday, July 12
Distance: 73.343 km to Moncton, NB

After an early morning snack of a delicious bakery-made granola bar and fruit, I got on the bike to cross the Cocagne Bridge. I took the small secondary road 535 and reached Notre Dame in no time, but with no breakfast stop available, I just did some stretching and carried on. In Irishtown, I stopped at the first Timmy's for coffee and breakfast and studied the maps. I took Hwy 115 to Route 2 (the TC Hwy) and headed west into the city, taking exit 454 to the Camper City campground. Moncton was busy due to the very popular Atlantic Nationals car show. This is Canada's largest annual car show event and I just happened to be in Moncton that weekend. That made accommodations in Moncton very scarce.

When I reached the bustling campground, the poor owner was trying to assist a lineup of customers and there was an inexperienced assistant who was not much help. I accepted the only camping spot available at the time, set up among many large recreational vehicles and then wandered the large campground looking for a more appropriate site. There seemed to be one available tent site so I lined up again and received permission from the proprietor to move to it. An assistant with a golf cart was sent around to help me move my gear. I cycled along while he moved my tent and panniers on his cart to a treed area with neighbouring small tents. My tent handily fit into this campsite community. I familiarized myself with directions to town and the airport and started touring around Moncton.

Often, the roads and maps in an urban area are difficult to understand. I stopped at a Hyundai dealer to make sure I was on the correct route. Strangely, the first salesman I talked to did not even understand how to read a map! After receiving directions from a different fellow, I cycled into town and the TIC for maps and a list of things to do. The Moncton Market was just about to close down when I found it so I quickly scurried in to buy food. I enjoyed the Moncton museum and a secondhand bookstore where I purchased a new (used) book. Back at the campsite, there was time for a quick swim at the busy pool and a nice hot shower. In the change room, I noticed another woman with cycling tan lines and realized it was Carmel, the cross-Canada cyclist whom I had not seen since those supremely windy days in Saskatchewan. We chatted about schedules and challenges. We discussed meeting again in the evening, but we never did cross paths again.

Day 74, Sunday, July 13
Distance: 60 km along Route 15 to Shediac, NB

I left about 7:30 am from Camper City, stopped for a long breakfast at Timmy's then took Rte 15 to the airport, reaching there around 9:30 am. I talked to the TIC staff at the airport about routes and cycling, while waiting for the flight from Toronto. The WestJet flight from Victoria/Toronto was on time—YAHOO! My emotions were all over the place as I waited excitedly to greet Susan, Denise, Kerri (friends from Victoria) and especially Naomi (my daughter)! When they actually physically walked down the ramp towards the waiting area, both parties were elated! What a feeling of relief that all the crew made it. When I was able to lay eyes on my daughter, Naomi, we were both ecstatic. We hugged until we cried. It had been months since we had last seen each other and there was further hugging and chatting while waiting for the bicycles to arrive in the luggage area. We experienced more relief when the bicycles actually arrived safe and sound, in their clear plastic bags. The dynamics of being in a group were very different from being alone. Even putting the bikes back together as a group was lively. We took over a section of the airport, much to the entertainment of various onlookers.

Finally we were on our way, tentatively at first to make sure the bicycles were fine. Kerri initially had a gear issue, but it was fixable and resolved shortly thereafter. There were many photo stops, especially at the airport sign, displaying Moncton International.

We stopped at the local Timmy's, so conveniently located beside the airport, as everyone needed food and drink. Cycling the 20 km along Rte 15 east to Shediac, we noticed a surprising amount of porcupine roadkill, not seen (or else not noticed) elsewhere in Canada. With the strong tailwind and fine weather, we soon reached the giant lobster, symbol of Shediac, a tribute to the crustacean. There was a lone touring cyclist there with whom I could sympathize, as we all took photos of each other. We were willing and able to cycle further towards the Confederation Bridge, but we had reserved a campground site at Shediac and there were no refunds, unfortunately. We had planned the reservation in case the group had jet lag from their overnight flight from Victoria, but they certainly did not seem tired. Susan was the resident Girl Guide and was nicknamed "Bossy Owl", as she knew how to plan and how to action the plan.

We had plenty of time for a swim in the pool, to get cleaned up and cycle into town for a delicious lobster meal. Being with the group made it a lot more enjoyable.

Day 75, Monday, July 14
Distance: 100 km to Victoria, PEI, 42 km to
Confederation Bridge in NB, 58 km in PEI

We woke at 6:00 am to get an early start as we knew this would be a long day, cycled to Cap-Pelé and to Timmy's for breakfast and extras for lunch. We discovered Denise's knack for asking directions from strangers and nicknamed her "Asking Owl". We cycled on the road through town and bought some fruit for later. The road met up with Rte 15 and we cycled on that road all the way to the Confederation Bridge. We met up with Bob and Joan, who joked that this new group must've brought the rain. I introduced my friends to Bob and Joan and commented about cycling with a group being a different experience from cycling on my own.

Denise, Kerri, Naomi, Susan and I waiting for the shuttle across the Confederation Bridge from NB to PEI; Day 75

The rain began early and continued our entire ride to the bridge. We reached the bridge terminal at about 12:30 pm sopping wet. We all used the washrooms, trying to dry off using the hand dryers. While waiting for the shuttle bus to take us across the bridge, we ate our lunch of fruit and chatted with Bob and

Joan while still attempting to dry off. The usual large van was not operational so we were transported by two trucks. The bicycle trailer was wonderful, strapping bicycles on with Velcro straps and managing to fit all seven bicycles alternating front wheel to back wheel.

The Confederation Bridge is an amazing feat of engineering. The length is 12.5 km with no side rails, so it would be horrendous to cross on a bicycle. Built in 1997, it has only closed four times for snow or weather. The shuttle buses are an excellent, safe and dry mode of transport and a good way to view the bridge. Our shuttle bus driver told us stories about the bridge and a couple of folks who attempted to cross the bridge illegally on foot.

Once safely across to PEI and a new province, we retrieved our bikes and loaded our gear back on. We cycled in the sprinkling rain along the TC Hwy 2 to Rte 10, a secondary road (part of the Blue Heron Coast Drive), towards Hampton. The group was pleased to retreat from the busy TC Hwy to more rural routes through the rolling Prince Edward Island countryside. We were only lost once. Susan lost a pannier on one section of a very rough bridge, but luckily I was behind her and saw it escape.

We stopped at Victoria, PEI to take photos of the sign (as we were all from Victoria, BC) and got directions to Denise's friend's abode. We had to cycle north to the main highway then south down a long lane back towards the ocean, near Victoria but separated by an inlet of water. Cycling the long day was worth it, as it led to the ocean-side cottage owned by Denise's friend, Margaret. There was a small bunkhouse where Susan and Kerri slept. Naomi and I were fortunate to share a lovely bedroom in the main cottage. Denise bedded down on a couch in the sunroom. The ocean view was magnificent with the Confederation Bridge in the background.

We were so lucky to stay there. Margaret fed us appetizers, clams, fish, potatoes, salad, strawberries and wine to boot. After supper, we went for our first swim in the Atlantic Ocean. Margaret led the way and we finally joined her. We played Rooster, Turkey, Chicken, Duck to make us "duck" under the water. The water felt wonderful and warm in the lingering light. After the swim, we used a very unique private, outdoor shower beside Margaret's house to clean off the sweat and salt water. All of our gear was drying on clotheslines around the house. Unfortunately, Margaret had lost her glasses in the ocean. I told her I would be able to look for them underwater if I had a mask or goggles, but she was not able to find any. The rest of the group made fun of my cycling tan lines, quite visible when wearing a swimsuit.

New Brunswick Statistics

Distance: 473.3 km

Days: 5

Tent camping nights: 5

New Brunswick

Day	Km	Destination	Route	Notes
70	104.8	Nigadoo, NB	NB Hwy 134	coastline
71	85.53	Miramichi	NB Hwy 8	rolling hills
72	107.6	Cocagne	Hwy 11, Hwy 134	coastline
73	73.34	Moncton	Hwy 535, Hwy 115	rural, highway
74	60	Shediac, NB	Hwy 15	highway
75	42	Confederation Bridge	Hwy 15, Hwy 16, bridge	Confederation bridge
	473.3	**New Brunswick total kms**		

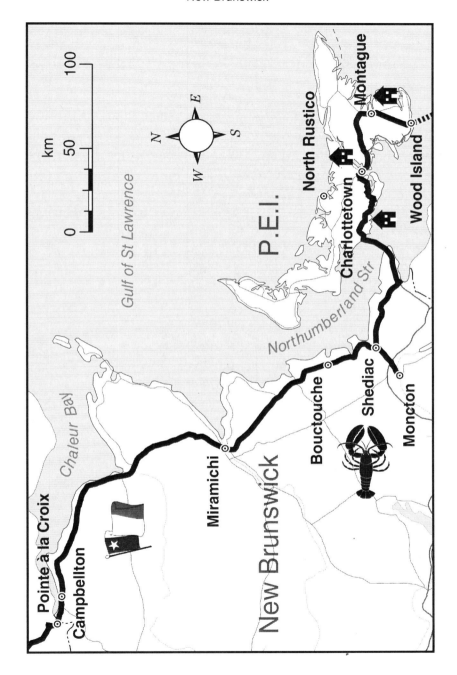

Day 76, Tuesday, July 15
Distance: 33 km along the TC Hwy 1 to Charlottetown

Everyone awoke at different times, not that it really mattered. I had to wake Naomi up at 9:00 am, so we could have breakfast and get moving. We tried to maintain our bikes after cycling the wet roads, lubing our chains and gears. It was an easy cycling day, returning to the highway and cycling the short distance to Charlottetown. Denise, who was born and grew up on PEI, knew the route and the town so we blindly followed her. It is so much less stressful to follow along someone who knows the route somewhat than to plot out each day's course. After leading us to meet an old boyfriend at his insurance firm, Denise then piloted us to a bicycle shop. We all needed to check our tire pressure and Kerri had to get her rear wheel straightened with a couple of new spokes. Naomi tried to add her own air and ended up blowing the valve when trying to remove the pump end. Luckily, the bike shop staff were easily able to replace the tube for us. We met Lorne and Meaghan, Denise's nephew and wife and joined them for a late lunch at JUGS (Just Us Girls, a fashion cafe). We thoroughly enjoyed being in the heart of downtown Charlottetown with some locals. Denise departed with Lorne and Meaghan to buy some lobster while Susan, Kerri, Naomi and I went touring downtown Charlottetown, including shopping at the Cows store, famous for its funny t-shirts. The town has many historic buildings, including the building where the Fathers of Confederation discussed joining together, resulting in Charlottetown being called Canada's Birthplace of Confederation.

We cycled to East Royalty and as we reached Lorne and Meaghan's house before they did, we took the dogs, Aussie and Nikita, out for a walk, had showers and settled into their

142

lovely home. One of their pieces of artwork on the living room wall was a painting of five cyclists, which seemed like an appropriate positive omen. Once again, I felt so lucky to be welcomed into someone's comfortable home.

When Denise and our hosts returned, they put on a big PEI spread of fresh local lobster, corn with local beer and wine. We were tickled to see that Meaghan had made a special cake topped with a bicycle design in icing! This was quite a social gathering, which carried on until early morning. I crashed about midnight, others were up until 2:00 am and Denise and our hosts were awake until 4:30 am!

Day 77, Wednesday, July 16
Distance: 0 km; rented a car to tour PEI

We rented a car from a contact of Lorne to see many of the PEI tourist sites in one quick day. Denise, not surprisingly, decided to have a rest day in the house. The rest of the group drove to the north shore of the island, through Brackley Point to the Green Gables tourist site. The tourism industry seemed

Lobster traps on PEI dock

to be sagging, since this was peak summer season and Green Gables was certainly not packed. There were lots of accommodation vacancy signs, as well. We tasted the local ice cream and shopped at a nearby Cows store for "seconds" near North Rustico. We stayed in the general vicinity to test out the beaches and water at Brackley Beach and at Prince Edward Island National Park. The sand really was red and the hot, sunny weather made for a pleasant beach day. The water was fine although there were many small jellyfish to watch out for. We swam anyway—very refreshing!

We met up with Denise and Meaghan and returned to the house, catching up on news on the Internet. Kerri was happily surprised as there was an email for her with a job offer back in BC. We eventually ate out at a Chinese restaurant in Charlottetown for supper. As this was our last night in Charlottetown, we were happy to spend it with our hosts, saying goodbye and thank you in the evening in case we missed seeing them in the morning.

Day 78, Thursday, July 17
Distance: 50 km mainly along Hwy 3 to Brudenell, PEI

A 7:30 am start allowed us to avoid the heat of the day, beginning with a cycle across the Hillsborough River Bridge to Stratford and a stop at Timmy's for coffee and breakfast. We cycled along the TC Hwy 1 past the red potato fields and picturesque agricultural scenes, stopping for several photo

Water stop on the way to
Brudenell; Day78
(photo: S.Zedel)

breaks. At the Cherry Valley intersection, we took Hwy 3 to Brudenell, where we cycled along a very red dirt trail, part of the Confederation Trail, near Pooles Corner. Denise grew up in this neighbourhood and she took us past her family home.

We arrived at Denise's friend, Tanya's, home and were once again met by Lorne and Meaghan who had arrived in their vehicles. We dropped off our bicycles and gear, grabbed our boating and swimming gear and hopped into their vehicles. They drove us to East

Point at the very northeast tip of the Island. There were several new wind generators, which makes sense with the strong winds there. The boat cruise on Lorne and Meaghan's the "Good Enough" lobster fish boat was exhilarating. They process their catch at the world's largest lobster processing plant nearby on PEI. We felt so fortunate to be on a private boat on the Atlantic Ocean with fresh lobster sandwiches, wonderful sunny weather, good company and the scenic east coast of PEI as a backdrop. We were truly experiencing PEI life, searching for whales on a lobster boat.

As there were no whales to be seen, we headed back to land and were toured next to Basin Head, a provincial park with magnificent sandy beaches. The most entertaining activity there was the Basin Head run. Swimmers who had enough courage would jump off a dock, dropping several metres into the deep ocean to be swept out to the shallows via tidal current. Only certain of our group did not have the courage, as the thrill of the jump and the amusement of running out to sea was worth trying more than once. When walking back to the dock, the swimmer walked along the "singing sands" beach, where the white sand "sang" making unique squeaky sounds.

Lorne and Meaghan then drove us back to Tanya's where we cleaned off the salt and sweat, and enjoyed a meal of scallops, roast

Basin Head jumping spot; Day 78
(photo: S. Zedel)

chicken and veggies followed by strawberries and whipped cream. Lorne and Meaghan had to return to Charlottetown, so we said a quick goodbye and thank you to them on their departure. The rest of us went out to a Ceilidh (kay-lee), an evening of music and dancing. This event was held in the local Bingo Hall, filled to the rafters with all generations of spectators. Tanya took us there with her grandchildren and everyone seemed to know everyone else. The most amazing thing was someone knew me! Wendy W. from my office in Victoria saw me and we both screamed in amazement! She was touring around by car, but we did not know we were in the same area as both our Blackberrys were out of commission (or *lost*). The fiddlers/guitarists/singers were from nearby on PEI and Cape Breton and an amazing step dancer also graced the crowded stage at one point. The music was excellent and some of the cyclists bought Tim Chiasson and Fiddler's Sons CDs for souvenirs. The performance was like an old time radio show where plugs for the local bakery, butcher, tire shop and beauty salon were announced between sets. Homemade fudge was sold at the break, but since Tanya had made and brought her own, we were already enjoying snacking on delicious fudge during the show (recipe at the back). Tanya brought us back to her house where we chatted and were all able to sleep in very comfortable beds.

Day 79, Friday, July 18
Distance: 120 km to Antigonish, 25 km in Prince Edward Island, 95 km in Nova Scotia

We woke up at about 6:30 am to have a quick breakfast at Tanya's and get on the road early to ensure we caught the 9:30 am Wood Islands ferry. PEI folks seem to buy their coffee at coffee shops, so we had difficulty finding a coffee maker at the homes we stayed in. We said a huge thank you and goodbye to Tanya, as she had been a splendid host. We cycled to rolling Rte 315 straight south to the Wood Islands ferry terminal. There were no mileage signs, but it was about 30 km

Lining up for the ferry from PEI to Nova Scotia

and we were moving! We just caught the ferry and were not impressed with the ferry bike unfriendliness. The workers did not know where bicycles were to park, made Naomi move more than once, had no racks, made us strap our bicycles to the deck with unwieldy belts and wanted us to remove our panniers. We barely had enough time to eat as the ferry had no warning docking announcement. The ferry ride was only about an hour and we had thought it was an hour and a half. When we got close to docking, a worker came around and told us we were docking in a few minutes. We were not pleased as we had to rush to get below deck, release our bikes and prepare for

Sign in Pictou County, NS

cycling again! We were so used to the efficiency of BC Ferries.

The ferry arrived in Pictou, NS, already province number three for the new group. The tour of PEI had been quick as we toured the province in only four days. We cycled to the Pictou TIC, got somewhat oriented, then cycled over a causeway to New Glasgow where we stopped at Sobey's for snacks, fruit and drinks. Kerri was again experiencing tire rim problems as more spokes were breaking and her rear tire was still wobbling. We were luckily fairly close to a bike shop, so we cycled there and waited while the staff replaced Kerri's rear wheel totally. Her new wheel was an unexpected souvenir of Nova Scotia. While waiting, the rest of us enjoyed relaxing out of the sun.

We resumed along hilly secondary road #4, which seemed to parallel the main TC Hwy 104 for quite a distance, without the busy traffic. There was nowhere to stop and rest so we had a snack break along the side of the road. We eventually merged onto the TC Hwy as it seemed to be a more direct route to Antigonish, our destination. Antigonish (a Micmac name meaning Five Forked Rivers of Fish) was built where the rivers converge.

The group was getting tired and anxious to arrive at the accommodation that Susan had pre-booked at Antigonish. We pulled into the St. Francis Xavier University (StFX) grounds around 6:30 pm. Poor Susan. The registration desk was not very organized and made several errors. They handed her two security pass cards to enter the buildings and rooms. She had to return to the office (on bicycle as it was not really close) twice because they had messed up the codes. The dorms themselves were fine. We were able to secure our bicycles and gear inside and have excellent hot showers in clean facilities. We were unsure of where to eat so we wandered on foot down a nearby street and eventually found a strip of restaurants. The group had a tough time deciding which of four mediocre restaurants to choose from, but we finally got some food and drink. We returned to our dorms for a night's sleep in a real bed again.

Prince Edward Island Statistics

Distance: 166 km
Days: 4, including 1 rest day
Home accommodation: 4 nights

Prince Edward Island				
Day	**Km**	**Destination**	**Route**	**Notes**
75	58	Victoria, PEI	small roads	rural
76	33	Charlottetown, PEI	Hwy 1 (TC Hwy)	rural
77	0	around PEI	touring PEI	rental vehicle drive
78	50	Brudenell	Hwy 3	boat tour
79	25	Wood Island ferry	Hwy 315	rural
	166	**Prince Edward Island total kms**		

Day 80, Saturday, July 19
Distance: 103 km to Whycocomagh, NS

The Antigonish Highland Games were starting that Saturday, which is why Susan had pre-booked the accommodations. We stayed to watch the Games parade that was beginning at the StFX University grounds. Susan, Kerri, Naomi and I walked to Timmy's to purchase breakfast then carried it to the parade route. We sat on the road curb and ate our breakfast from front row seats. The parade started about 9:00 am and included many marching pipe bands, classic cars, dressed-up car floats and clowns giving out candy, which we shared with nearby children. All in all, it was very entertaining and finished around 9:30 am. We found Denise and returned to the dorm to pack up for a new day on the road. We cycled along the main TC Hwy, Rte 104, past mostly rolling hills with spruce forest to the Canso Causeway. This is a very narrow causeway for road and rail (the world's deepest causeway) crossing the Strait of Canso to Cape Breton Island. Stopping just before crossing, someone started singing *Farewell to Nova Scotia*, with everyone joining in the chorus. That was enough to make Naomi depart for the bridge. We all followed suit, but the bridge was not designed for bicycle travelers. It nearly left Denise on the wrong side of the strait, as she was too worried for her safety and was not about to cross that bridge on bicycle. We took some photos of the "Welcome to Cape Breton Island" sign before Denise and I tentatively made the crossing.

We met at the TIC at Port Hawkesbury on the Cape Breton Island side of the Causeway and ate an excellent seafood chowder lunch at the Sky Lodge there. The day's cycle was up and down rolling hills then through some construction where the top layer of asphalt was being removed. The road was bumpy enough that my cycle computer unfortunately decided to jump off. At that point, the odometer from Mile 0 in Victoria was about 6,540, but that may not have been entirely accurate. I noticed the odometer missing when we reached the bottom of the hill of construction and it was not enough incentive for me to return up the hill to look for it.

We cycled to the first town with a campsite on our way to the Cape Breton Highlands. This was at Whycocomagh, a wonderful Gaelic name. Upon entering Cape Breton, we noticed signs and posters in English and Gaelic. Gaelic was

Kerri, Denise, Susan and I posing by the
Whycocomagh sign; Day 80

not heard on the street, but there must be interest in keeping the language alive here, as classes to learn Gaelic abound. We set up camp, had showers and headed off to eat. We came to the realization that no restaurants were open in the tiny community at that late hour of about 8:00 pm. We went to the local gas station and bought chips, salsa, cereal, milk and a can of beans. We managed to concoct a dinner and eat in the community room at the campsite. Kerri had us drink V-8 juices for our liquid salad. While searching for dinner utensils, someone found a stash of beer hidden in a cupboard. We decided to down a few, along with our juice, which added to our nutrition!

As it was Saturday night in Cape Breton, a dance was being held at the campsite. Our group of socialites definitely had to check that out. The dance was held in the camp picnic shelter; all picnic tables were filled with campers. There was a clearing, adequate for dancing, at the front where the DJ was announcing the CDs being played. When Naomi saw a fellow dancing with a broom, she was not about to stay, so she and I headed back to the community room to hang out. We could hear the *YMCA* and *Makarena* songs but no other songs that she recognized. Denise, Kerri and Susan stayed at the dance for a while longer.

Day 81, Sunday, July 20
Distance: 48 km to Baddeck, NS

Some of us were awoken early by noisy "trailer park boys" neighbours blaring ACDC from their Trans-Am. I returned to the community room to try to use the computer. The doors were locked, but the windows were not so I crawled in through an unlocked window to catch up on emails and my blog while the others slept. When everyone woke up, we went to Vy's Restaurant for breakfast. While there, Denise started talking to a construction worker and gave him the story of my cycling computer falling off. In the end, we asked him if he would mind giving me a ride back up to the road construction to see if we might possibly find the little computer. Naomi came with me and he was nice enough to slow down to a bare minimum to maximize our viewing ability. We really looked, but it was extremely difficult to spot a small bit of grey metal among the grey gravel. We tried our hardest to find it, but it was, unfortunately, not to be found. The computer was to have recorded the distance of the entire trip, including extra tours to town, so it was disappointing to have lost it. The construction worker took us back to the restaurant, so kind and apologetic. Naomi and I finished off our breakfast, then we all went next door to the bakery to buy some cookies and snacks, packed up and left the campsite by about noon.

It was a very pleasant cycle: rolling hills, slight breeze, comfortable temperature, beautiful scenery and quite a short distance. At one point along the highway, we noticed a message written onto the pavement in chalk: "**GO, PATTI!**" We figured it was probably Bob and Joan who must have been ahead of us. Such a unique idea and what a surprise to see! We reached the Bras d'Or Lakes campground by about 2:00 pm. It is near Baddeck, the start/end of the Cabot Trail that encircles Cape Breton Highlands National Park. The campground was well equipped with a pool and laundry facilities. We set up camp, did laundry and had a refreshing swim in the pool. As the tenting neighbours were few and we had many items to air dry, we hung our laundry on makeshift clotheslines in the small kitchen shelter by all our tents. We cycled the 5 km to the village of Baddeck and visited the Alexander Graham Bell Museum. Bell was an amazing man for his time, had a second home and spent a lot of time near Baddeck. Watching the videos was interesting but nearly put some of us to sleep so we had to keep moving along. Bob and Joan were on the same agenda, so we chatted and found out that they had left the chalk message on the pavement.

We stopped and shopped in town, then went out for an excellent dinner at the Linwood with lobster, salad and lasagna along with live music—very nice. By the time we cycled back to the campsite, it was nearly dark. Denise had gone her own way to a Ceilidh, but thank goodness she returned safely back to the campsite under the cover of the night.

Day 82, Monday, July 21
Distance: 56 km along Hwy 105, rolling hills to North Sydney, NS

We had an early shower around 7:00 am and packed. The rain overnight had soaked the tent, but luckily the laundry and our panniers were under cover and still dry. After cycling to Baddeck, we stopped first for banking, then on to a cafe for breakfast bagels and coffee. The cafe had excellent baked goods so we bought extra cookies and muffins for the road, stopping at the Co-op for yogurt, fruit and other snacks. We finally left and cycled the 8% grade to the top of Kelly's Mountain (summit about 240 m). The climb was long and steady and the mist and rain made it difficult to REALLY see any good views. In Nova Scotia, they have "lookoffs" where the rest of the country has "lookouts" so we tried to look off without riding off the cliff side!

We donned our jackets for the 8% grade descent to the bottom of the "mountain" that descended to the Seal Island Bridge. The Bridge crosses the Seal Island Inlet, an inland sea. The bridge was quite a feat built in 1960-61, adding a vital link to TC Hwy 105 making Cape Breton more easily accessible. Unfortunately, back in the 1960s, the engineers did not consider a lane for bicycles or pedestrians. After traversing the bridge, we stopped for fruit and yogurt and discovered oatcakes and Johnny cakes at the rest stop. Oatcakes are to the Scottish and Nova Scotians what baguettes are to the French. We sampled the local specialty foods whenever possible. As everyone was soaked through, we carried on to avoid getting too chilled. We turned off at the Arm of Gold campground amidst the continuing rain. The torrential downpour was apparently the tail end of a tropical storm. Luckily for us, there was a cabin available for rent. We shared the cabin and used the camp facilities: hot showers, laundry, table tennis tables,

Jacuzzi baths and the shared kitchen area. Kerri, Naomi and I caught a ride to the Avis rental car office in North Sydney so we could pick up the rental van that Susan had reserved. With the van, it was easy to shop for groceries and wine and haul it all back to the campsite. As the rain continued to pour down, Naomi and I slept in the van to make it easy the next morning.

Day 83, Tuesday, July 22
Distance: 0 km, rented a car to tour Cape Breton

By 7:00 am, we were changed and moving the seats back into the van. Kerri drove and we all settled in for a touring day off the bicycles, a welcome respite since it was still pouring rain. We stopped at Robin's to grab a coffee and ate leftover oatcakes and snacks. Our drive took us back along the TC Hwy west toward Baddeck and then north towards the Cabot Trail. The rain became misty and then lighter as we drove farther north. We even saw blue sky as we headed farther north and west.

The Cabot Trail loops around the entire northern tip of Cape Breton Island, including the Cape Breton Highlands National Park. The park preserves the highlands plateau with

Cape Breton Highlands National Park
(photo: S. Zedel)

its steep cliffs, stunning views of the Atlantic Ocean and rare and endangered plant and animal life. There are many communities along the trail, with numerous arts and crafts people and shops. We drove the entire Cabot Trail, making stops at various artisan shops to view sewing, jewelry, pewter, pottery, hooked rugs and other Cape Breton craft items. Knowing we would have to pack and carry any purchased item may have reduced our spending. We all enjoyed the day being able to stop whenever we wanted. Lunch was seafood and hot soup at a restaurant near Ingonish. Nearby, we stopped to walk along a stretch of beach with huge waves of murky green water. The day was still grey and cool, not conducive to playing on the beach, but there was quite a lovely vista of the ocean and surrounding area. We took numerous photo stops trying to capture the breathtaking scenery with a camera.

We returned the car and got a drive back to the campsite from Pearl, who worked at the car rental agency. Kerri, Susan and Denise found a small restaurant to eat a home-style dinner. At the campground tuck shop, Naomi and I bought veggies and fish and chips that we ate in the community room, where we tried to dry the tents while playing table tennis. As the rain was ongoing, Naomi and I showered, packed and slept in the cabin with the rest of the gang, to make the morning tasks easier.

Day 84, Wednesday, July 23
Distance: 5 km to Marine Atlantic ferry terminal, ferry to Argentia, NS

We woke early and packed as we had to cycle to the Marine Atlantic ferry terminal at North Sydney by 7:00 am. The cars were lined up in huge queues, and after a confusing entry to the terminal, we found the cyclists queued up on their own. Besides the five of us, there were Joan and Bob from Kamloops, Derrek and C from "Deconstructing Dinner" and Jan from Belgium, all who were on their last leg of cycling across the country. How amazing that such a disparate bunch of cyclists would meet together on this ferry trip! At that time in 2008, cost of the ferry was $89 for each passenger plus $28 for the bicycle. Strangely, the ferry crew did not know where to park the bicycles. It took some arguing between crew members to find a safe spot for the bicycles separate from the cars, which were also taking a long time to park.

We finally got our bikes parked but were told we had to carry enough supplies with us to last the entire seventeen-hour voyage, as passengers were not allowed to go below deck once the ship started. We brought a small amount of gear, including Gravol for possible seasickness, as we had seen video of the ship at sea. We were finally able to go above to the passenger deck and find a base spot for our gear. We bought coffee, muffins and yogurt and chatted with the other cyclists, as well as other fellow passengers. The other cyclists all had interesting anecdotes to share about their cross-Canada tour. All the cyclists were on independent tours with flexible schedules, and we had all chosen to take the long ferry from Nova Scotia to Argentia to reach our final destination of St. John's in Newfoundland in the last few days. Another option had been to take the short ferry to the very western coast of Newfoundland and cycle about 900 km across the province.

As it was a long ferry ride, Naomi and I toured the ship to see what other activities were available: a movie in the theatre at a set time, live entertainment in the pub at certain times and food in the cafeteria only available at set times. We also researched the reason that the schedule said 14-15 hours. Susan had been told about twelve hours and this trip was actually more than seventeen hours. We discovered that only three of four engines were operating and it had been that way for the past several months.

Naomi and I had some soup, which made us appreciate BC Ferries' clam chowder, then we sat down in the movie theatre to watch *21*. The theatre was large enough for 50 or so passengers and was very comfortable. The seats leaned back and had leg rests—handy for sleeping in once the movie was finished! The crowd was mostly teenagers and young adults, some were rugby teammates.

After the movie, we played rummy while talking to some neighbours. Some folks were Japanese Canadians from Toronto who may know my extended Kagawa family through the Japanese United Church there.

When the cafeteria was actually open, Naomi and I went to feast on a Mr. Sub sandwich. We sat and chatted with Bob and Joan, who were old friends now, and Jan from Belgium. Jan had a video camera and GPS unit mounted on his bike and carried a laptop and many other accessories. As Jan was from outside the country, he had interesting perspectives on Canada and cycling in this country. He thought Canada's melting pot society seemed to work more naturally than some European immigration policies.

Naomi went to watch a TV movie while I socialized with Denise, Susan and Kerri in the pub. There were some UK rugby team coaches who were pubbing as well, providing as much entertainment as the live music. I then tried to catch some sleep in the now-empty theatre, where seats were more comfortable than the regular seats.

Finally, the ferry docked at Argentia in Newfoundland at an uncivilized 2:30 am! We had to get our bikes all packed up and lit up for a night ride to the B&B that Susan had booked. Climbing the steep hill from the ferry terminal at 3:00 am in the ebony darkness, not really knowing where we were going, with trucks streaming off the ferry was not the most pleasant ride. I was mainly following in Denise's bright lights as my front headlights were too dull for the deep black and foggy night air. Thank goodness the poor hosts knew we were arriving at that late hour and were ready for us, as we poured into their rooms and beds. By then, it was 3:45 am, now into Newfoundland time zone, a half hour later than Atlantic Time and 4½ hours later than BC's Pacific Time zone! What an introduction to another province!

Nova Scotia Statistics

Distance: 302 km
Days: 5, including 1 rest day
Tent camping nights: 4
Student accommodation: 1

Nova Scotia

Day	Km	Destination	Route	Notes
79	95	Antigonish, NS	Hwy 4, 104 (TC Hwy)	rolling hills
80	103	Whycocomagh	Hwy 105	hilly, major bridge
81	48	Baddeck	Hwy 105	hilly
82	56	North Sydney	Hwy 105	rolling hills
83	0	Cape Breton island	touring Cape Breton	rental vehicle drive
84	5	Marine Atlantic ferry terminal		ferry ride
	307	Nova Scotia total kms		

Cycling the Maritimes

Cycling through New Brunswick, Nova Scotia and Prince Edward Island with its rolling terrain, friendly people and smaller towns makes cycling there enjoyable for all. The roads may not be as well suited for bicycles, but the lower population densities of these areas results in reduced car traffic. In general, cycling is still growing as a mode of transit in these provinces, where the touring cyclist is regarded as an oddity. The charming residents of the Maritime Provinces, both friends and strangers, win over the tourists to make them feel at home.

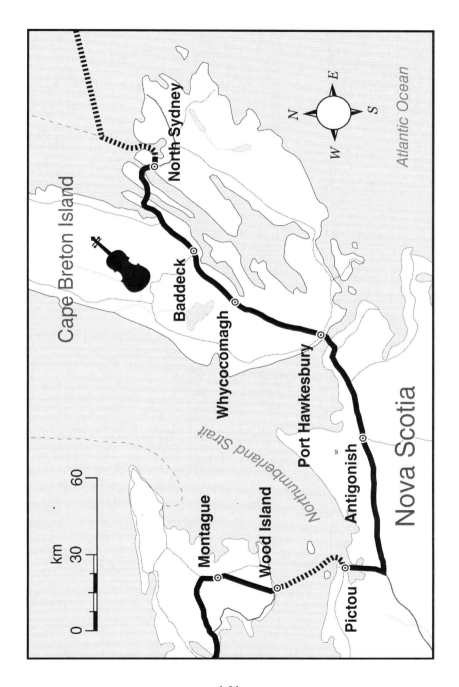

Day 85, Thursday, July 24
Dist: 100.22 to Butter Pot Provincial Park, NF

Everyone was bagged, of course, after such a short night's rest. Breakfast was provided until 10 am so I managed to wake them all up for breakfast by about 9:45 am. We packed and were on the road again heading out past Argentia-Whitburne. At that point, there were nice wide shoulders and very little traffic as the ferry was the end of that road. The cycling was quite enjoyable with a few good uphills and several long downhills. Poor Naomi really needed sleep, like all teenagers. She had a headache so we stopped, gave her some juice and Tylenol, added sunscreen and she managed to carry on, like the trooper that she is!

At the turnoff to Whitburne, we caught up to Bob and Joan and chatted. We were also passed by Jan, with his video camera and other equipment hanging off various parts of his bike. He'd had an amazing adventure, nearly always camping, rarely in an authorized campground. We stopped at the TIC and were given St. John's and camping information. I was able to call Glenda, wife of Mark (my husband's brother and host in St. John's) to keep her posted—excellent to talk to her.

We stopped for a real lunch at the Esso Monty's restaurant. Denise had a test of another poutine. The rest of us had sandwiches, drinks and pie and then we purchased fruit, tortillas and beans at Food Express for our final camping meal.

The terrain was getting more rugged and the vegetation changing to boreal forest with many bogs. Back to boreal forest meant back to increasing numbers of bothersome bugs, including some nasty horseflies. We stopped for a rest break at a site with few trees, sparse vegetation and random boulders strewn about looking like a moonscape.

After a few more water and stretch breaks, we cycled to Butter Pot Provincial Park, about 30 km from St. John's. Butter Pot refers to a specific rounded hill located within the park boundaries. The provincial park was beautiful, with a swimming area and comfort stations with showers, and was forested with black spruce, balsam fir and tamarack trees. After a swim and shower, we ate a late dinner of cheese tortillas while darkness approached.

Day 86, Friday, July 25
Distance: 40 km to Mile 0, St. John's, NF

Naomi slept in a bit while the rest of the group went visiting for coffee. This final cycling day was pleasant—warm but not too hot, a slight breeze, some very long downhills, a few uphills but a decent road and light traffic. We met Bob and Joan on the road near the final exit 41A to Hwy 2 into St.

TC Hwy in NF
(photo: S. Zedel)

John's. All of us, but especially Bob, Joan and I were excited at the prospect of reaching our final destination. My destination was Mile 0 in St. John's, NF and to meet up with Glenda, Mark and Karla. We were getting fired up knowing that this was our last day of cycling. Little did we know that that was to be our last meeting with Bob and Joan. We stopped at Timmy's for lunch and finally got a call through to Mark, my brother-in-law, deciding to meet at Mile 0 in town.

Mark and Karla (my 16-year-old niece) reached Mile 0 before us, so instead of waiting for us, Mark cycled out to meet us. Such a strange sight to see him appear on the highway cycling uphill toward us. I was at the tail end of our group of cyclists, so I had to try to get Naomi, Kerri, Denise and Susan

163

to understand to stop and wait for him. Mark came over to our side of the highway, met the crew and led the parade into downtown St. John's to the Mile 0 marker, where Karla was waiting.

As we cycled through the capital of the province, I was remembering the beginning of the trip, at Mile 0 in Victoria. It seemed like so long ago and yet, it seemed like the day before. Had three months really passed since the start? We easily reached the Mile 0 sign situated in downtown St. John's, signifying the end of the tour. Mainly, I felt an overwhelming sense of relief and accomplishment at finishing the journey with no major disasters. I realized that any challenge can be met by working at it step by step or one day at time. The thrill of achieving my challenge was shared with all the friends and family present. The triumphant feeling grew as we took photos of each other and gave congratulations all around at the Mile 0 marker. Mark and Karla courteously waited while we talked about our accomplishment and need to touch the ocean.

Mile 0 marker at St. John's NF with Susan, Naomi, Kerri and Denise

Next stop was the Atlantic Ocean, which we figured would be right there in the harbour. Apparently, there is a lot of lore about what lurks in the harbour, so we kept going further. Mark led us up, down and around a small lake along the waterfront to Quidi Vidi Village, a very picturesque and historic fishing village. We dipped a hand into the

Atlantic Ocean, then clinked and drank some Quidi Vidi beers (which someone had secretly carried along) to toast the end of the journey! The view of the historic village and the rugged shoreline was very east coast, looking nothing like the west coast we were familiar with. The Quidi Vidi brewery was right in the village and we were able to return empty bottles there.

We cycled to a point where the Zedel crew (Denise, Kerri

Mile 0 marker at St.John's, NF; Day 86

and Susan) split away to cycle to their host, Susan's brother-in-law. Mark, Karla, Naomi and I took the high road through the Legislative Assembly grounds to Mark and Glenda's lovely home on a quiet road in a comfortable neighbourhood. We showered and did laundry while Mark went to pick up the Zedel crew for a BBQ back at his home.

Glenda's mom came by for a quick visit to say hello before Glenda had to drive her to the airport. The newly-renovated kitchen in the large house received much traffic that evening and over the next week. We all enjoyed an excellent meal of wonderful salad, garlic toast, all kinds of burgers, chicken and lots of stories.

Newfoundland Statistics

Distance: 140.22 km
Days: 2
Camping night: 1
Ferry ride: 17 hours including part of a night
Home accommodation: 1 night

Newfoundland

Day	Km	Destination	Route	Notes
85	100.22	Butter Pot Prov Park	Hwy 100, 1 (TC Hwy)	hilly
86	40	Mile 0, St John's NF	Hwy 1 (TC Hwy)	final day!
	140.22	**Newfoundland total kms**		

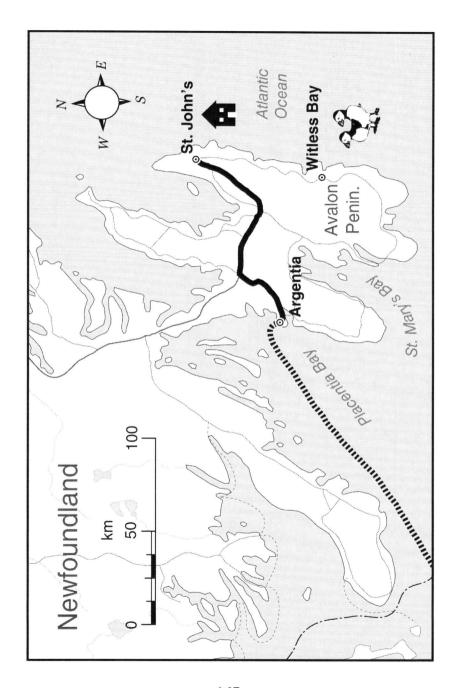

Saturday, July 26: Cape Spear

Naomi and I were lucky to be able to stay with Mark and Glenda in their lovely home in St. John's after reaching Mile 0. Denise, Susan and Kerri stayed with Susan's brother-in-law at their home.

The next day, Naomi was very pleased to be off the saddle and able to travel via car to various tourist locations. Susan, Kerri and Denise also had a day to tour around via the brother-in-law's car. St. John's is Canada's oldest city, full of brightly-coloured houses and buildings built right against and onto the rocky slopes. Mark drove us to Cape Spear, the most easterly point of North America. At the top is an amazing view of the city of St. John's, as well as the Atlantic Ocean coast.

After dinner in the evening, there was a final celebration of several touring cyclists who had finished a cross-Canada cycling tour on nearly the same day. The plan was to meet at Club One, one of the hottest venues on George. George Street has a reputation as the street with the most bars in North America. Naomi and Karla, being under-age, were unfortunately not able to join in the celebration. Glenda and I got as dressed up as we could and Mark drove us to Club One. Susan, Denise and Kerri were easy to spot on the dance floor, as were the four "Typically Canadian" cyclists who had also just crossed Canada and who organized this celebration. It felt like a true celebration of our collective efforts and it was wonderful to celebrate with good friends, as well as fellow cross-Canada cyclists.

At one point in the evening, someone called all cross-Canada cyclists up on stage, where I was forced to go up and say something. I didn't know what to say or do as I am not used to the limelight. En route to the mike, I chatted briefly with a few of the guys who coached me to say something or I would regret it forever. When it was my turn on stage, I announced who I was and said thank you to my friends who came to help me cycle to St. John's to finish the tour, announcing their names. Whew, I was glad to get down off the stage! I finally met Pierre, the guy that Joan and Bob kept telling me about, who was known as the 200 km-a-day guy. He eventually cycled over 11,000 km across the country, cycling the coast of the Gaspé Peninsula and entirely across Newfoundland. On his blog, he called me the "ghost," as he kept hearing stories about me and we kept missing each other (until that evening). Also in attendance were Derrick and C celebrating finishing their own tour. The only ones missing were Bob and Joan from Kamloops and Jan, the Belgian, who made it to St. John's and was travelling back to Belgium. How strange for eleven of us to start at various dates, travel different routes across the country, have our own agendas and still end up finishing our trips on pretty much the same date in St. John's, NF.

We hung out at Club One for quite a while, dancing, drinking, chatting and meeting various folks. Someone decided we needed to get "Screeched in," to fully engage in the St. John's folklore. This is a folk ceremony performed for non-Newfoundlanders by Newfoundlanders to welcome them to the province. Club One did not have the correct Screech (rum), so Denise, Kerri, Susan, Derrick, C, Glenda and I headed down George Street to another club that we were told did have the correct rum. We were just about to order at this very crowded folk club when—GIANT surprise—Mark showed up with my husband, Peter, at the bar! What a thrill to have him there to help celebrate and show support for this independent trip of mine. Everyone, including Peter, got their screech and got "Screeched in". Fortunately for us, there was no live cod to kiss (part of the formal ceremony). The live music was quite folksy at this bar, different than the dancing tunes of Club One. We were there chatting and drinking until the wee hours of the morning, quite an interesting, one-of-a-kind celebration. Mark was able to drive the Fuglem clan home and the Zedel clan back to their accommodation.

We spent another part of a week in Newfoundland, touring a bit beyond St. John's. Mark, Peter, Naomi, Karla and I took a boat trip out of Bay Bulls near Witless Bay to view the many whales that swarm around the area to feed. We also toured the Witless Bay Ecological Reserve to view the largest colony of puffins in North America. One evening, Glenda invited most of her eight siblings to dinner. One sister brought along a bakeapple pie, a prized Newfoundland specialty, with hand-picked bakeapple (berries). What a beautiful province and a wonderful ending to an amazing trip.

Entire Trip Statistics

Total number of days: 87
Total number of nights camping in a tent: 53
Total cycling kilometres: 6,302.62
Total riding days: 74
Average km per day: 85

Epilogue

After reflecting on this trip of a lifetime, I have concluded that I was so very lucky to be able to complete such an adventure. I was fortunate that the stars came together to allow me the luxury of having the needed time, money, energy, healthy body, healthy mind and especially the support of family and friends across the country. Thank you to all who helped make this journey happen and especially to Peter, Kai and Naomi.

References:

Lovett, Richard. 2001. Ragged Mountain Press/McGraw Hill. *The Essential Touring Cyclist, A Complete Guide for the Bicycle Traveler*, 2d edition.

Vélo Québec. 2006. *La Route Verte du Québec*. Guide officiel de l'itinéraire et des services—4e édition.

Wood, Paul A. 2006. Paul Wood Publishing. *Cycling British Columbia*.

Decisions, Decisions

Group tour, partners or solo. There are pluses and minuses for each type. If you like to meet people and enjoy camaraderie, group tours may be for you. These often have a support van to carry gear, help with meals, route planning and technical assistance. This translates into higher costs, less flexibility, finding a group tour that fits your schedule, timeframe and fitness level.

Solo gives one the most flexibility in scheduling, meals and accommodations and is likely cheapest but may be the most difficult mentally.

Partners who have similar fitness, daily distance, meal and touring needs are excellent if you can find those people wanting to join your tour.

For my trip, there were no group tours that fit my specific timeframe. I chose the option to plan for a solo trip with friends joining in various legs.

Type of bicycle. Touring bicycle frames are built for carrying fully-loaded front and back panniers, as well as the weight of you and all your gear. Your bike should have rivets for supports to carry panniers and water bottles and space for a handlebar bag. There are many adjustments that can be made so the bicycle you choose is properly fitted to your size, i.e. seat height/angle, handlebar stem/angle and many more. Make friends with your bike mechanic before heading off on tour. There was a lot of advice about bike frames, but for my weight of 52 kg, I decided to go for a lightweight aluminum frame.

Gearing and gear ratios. This needs to be considered to allow a low enough ratio for climbing any mountain and yet large enough to travel along flat terrain easily.

Type of tire. When considering the type of tire, the goal is to try to reduce the number of flat tires needing fixing at the side of the road. I highly recommend a very tough, puncture-resistant tire like Schwalbe's Marathon Plus. The width and type of tire will depend on your route—trail, gravel or pavement.

Type of panniers and other equipment. Panniers vs. trailer is a major decision. Pannier options to consider include volume, weight, waterproofness, compartments or pockets and especially rack fasteners. My front panniers are waterproof Ortlieb brand (25L) and my rear bags are Vaude (48L). The main considerations important to me are quality rack fasteners and light weight. Pannier specs and packing lists are at the back of the book. Instead of panniers, bike trailers also can be considered for carrying gear.

Handlebar bag. A handlebar bag that is easy to click on and off is an important accessory for ease of access to maps, snacks, camera, wallet and other essentials.

Hydration. The importance of hydration cannot be stressed enough. Most touring cyclists are fine with two mounted water bottles, although you can try the Camelbak system to see if that suits you.

Shoes and pedal systems. Clipless pedal systems like the SPD systems are recommended for cycling efficiency. Shoes with cleats should be chosen so that one can still walk around in town wearing them if necessary.

Route across Canada. This country is so large with many highways crossing it. The main highway that crosses the country is the Trans-Canada Hwy (TC Hwy 1). This highway is the main route that truckers and vehicles use to traverse the country so is not the most preferred for cyclists. I looked for a route off the TC Hwy; the route had to join up from province to province, be interesting, be safe, be less busy than the Trans-

Canada Highway and not go through major mountain passes and tunnels.

Maps and tourist information. I received these from each province after contacting their provincial tourist information website. The only province that did not send out a free map was British Columbia, my home province! Saskatchewan sent their tourist package out by courier and I got it within a day! Opening each package was interesting, viewing each province as a whole and then trying to determine a suitable cycling route.

Time of Year. May and June are quite optimal for cycling with longer days, fewer tourists and drivers and decent weather. It is preferred to travel in the off season for ease of camping and flexibility in planning accommodations.

Accommodations. Choices are many, with a huge range in comfort and price. It is a luxury to have flexibility so you can bed down where you end up cycling to each day (if there is no firm set schedule). The biggest luxury is to know friends en route and stay with them along the way. Camping is the most economical option, with campsites in most towns all across the country. Campground guides are available at TICs and change every year, so it is important to get up-to-date guides. If camping, there are many private campgrounds which are comparable in price to provincial parks with improved amenities (for cyclists) like laundry facilities, heated showers, washrooms with flush toilets and nearby restaurants or snack bars.

Cycling partners. Thank goodness for technology and the Internet. The World Wide Web became a good friend as I emailed former classmates from university, friends from underwater hockey (played this sport for about thirty years) and contacts of contacts all across the country. In the end, there were friends and contacts all across the country to cheer me on and give me accommodation, as well as a cycling partner in British Columbia and Alberta; in southern Ontario, Ottawa to Québec City and in the Maritimes; Moncton, NB to St. John's, NF. For some reason, no one wanted to cycle the prairies or northwest Ontario!

Speaking about technology and the Internet, there is certainly plenty of cycling information on the Internet. Type "cycle touring" into your search engine or check your local library for further information on technical details of cycle touring. For a list of gear I packed, please see Packing List at the back of this book.

My Final Choices

Bicycle: DeVinci Destination with Shimano gears

Panniers:
- Front panniers: waterproof Ortlieb Front Roller Plus, 25L, 1,300 g
- Rear panniers: Vaude Discover Pro, 48L with an extra 1L pocket, 1,700 g, very durable, polyester PU coated fabric, almost completely waterproof

Bicycle Handlebar bag: Detours Metro with a 'Klickfix' adaptor to easily attach/detach the bag to the handlebar

Tent: MEC Opera House 2; 2.2 kg (my main criteria); barely enough space for both Naomi and me but plenty of space for one person and gear

Sleeping Bag: my [35-year-old] Woods down sleeping bag with a silk sleeping bag liner and a Thermarest camp pillow

Tires: Schwalbe Marathon Plus

FAQ:

How many kilometres did you cycle in a day? Average of 85.

How much weight did you carry? About 50#; see packing list below

How much did it cost you? Budget a maximum $50/day: $20 for campsite, $30 for food and other needs

What kind of bicycle? DeVinci touring bike, see specs below

How many flat tires? Three until I changed tires to Schwalbe Marathon Plus

How long did it take you? About three months or 86 days

Have you bicycle toured before? Yes, maybe a week or so, at the end of travelling in Britain. No major long bicycle tours.

What's next? Maybe a different country. As I have roots and relatives in Japan, that would be a logical choice. I remember a 52-year-old Dutch man, whom I met in a hostel twenty years ago, who was cycle touring Japan and whom I would still like to emulate.

Packing List

Many items sorted into Ziploc bags for waterproofing, organizing and ease of finding

Handlebar bag: wallet, camera in its own case, micro energy lights, camera memory cards, Swiss army knife, lip balm, phone card, pen, notepaper, map(s)

Left Front Pannier: lock, utensils, one pot, duct tape, first aid kit with extra lotions

Right Front Pannier: trail food, i.e. granola bars, dried fruit and nuts, provincial maps, sunscreen, cotton bandanas, extra lock, toilet paper, compass, extra bungee cords, lights, cool max helmet liner

Left Rear
     Pannier: crocs (flexible shoes), cycling booties, batteries, bike parts, i.e. two tubes, spare tire, bike cleaning and lube kit, mini bike pump, journal, maps (not current), bathing suit, jerseys, polar fleece tights, base layer, extra jacket, sandals, small microfibre towel
     Pocket: headlamp, wind-up rechargeable bike light, MP3 player

Right Rear
     Pannier: camp pillow, large microfibre towel, book, batteries, chargers, underwear and socks, clothesline, contact lens kit, shampoo, conditioner, brush, extra cycling shorts, street wear, i.e. shorts, t-shirt
     Pocket: blackberry, extra glasses

On the bike: tent (two person), sleeping bag with silk liner within and stuffed in a waterproof stuff sack, camping thermarest mat, front and rear lights, two water bottles, cycle computer (until it jumped off)

Wearing: helmet with lights, glasses, fingerless full-fingered gloves, jersey, shorts, socks, bike shoes; when necessary: tights, waterproof jacket, and sometimes full-fingered gloves

_____

Tanya's Skor Bar Bits Fudge Recipe

3 c white sugar
¾ c butter
2/3 c evaporated milk
1 tsp vanilla
300 g milk choc chips

1 jar (7½ oz) Marshmallow
    Fluff
300 g pkg (or more) of Skor
    bar bits

In a large saucepan, combine sugar, butter, evaporated milk.
Bring to boil over low heat, stirring constantly, then boil 5 minutes.

Remove from heat;
Add: 1 tsp vanilla, 1 pkg milk choc chips.
Beat by hand until melted.

Add 1 jar of Marshmallow Fluff. Beat until blended.

Add ½ pkg of Skor bar bits or more.

Pour into greased 9" x 13" pan. Refrigerate.

About the Author

Patti is a professional forester, mother to Kai and Naomi, her children, and wife to Peter, a senior civil servant. She was born in Guelph, Ontario and lived in rural and urban Ontario and Alberta before moving to British Columbia, where she has lived for over thirty years. She works for the provincial government, who kindly gave her time off for this cycling excursion. She has always enjoyed sports, currently plays underwater hockey, and cycles 15 km to and from work. In 2008, when she was 52, she spent three months cycling across Canada, sometimes alone, often with partners.

Abbreviations Used in this Book:

B&B = bed and breakfast
CEGEP = *Collège d'enseignement général et professionnel* — a
Québec term that refers to a college in that province
GORP = good ol' raisins and peanuts (trail mix)
ha = hectares
hwy = highway
km = kilometres
kph = kilometres per hour
TIC = tourist information centre
Timmy's = Tim Horton's restaurant
TC Hwy = Trans-Canada highway